# Urban Growth Management Through Development Timing

David J. Brower
David W. Owens
Ronald Rosenberg
Ira Botvinick
Michael Mandel

foreword by
F. Stuart Chapin, Jr.

The Praeger Special Studies program—utilizing the most modern and efficient book production techniques and a selective worldwide distribution network—makes available to the academic, government, and business communities significant, timely research in U.S. and international economic, social, and political development.

# Urban Growth Management Through Development Timing

**Praeger Publishers** New York Washington London

PRAEGER SPECIAL STUDIES IN U.S. ECONOMIC, SOCIAL, AND POLITICAL ISSUES

Library of Congress Cataloging in Publication Data
Main entry under title:

Urban growth management through development timing.

  (Praeger special studies in U.S. economic, social, and
political issues)
  Includes bibliographical references and index.
  1. Cities and towns—Growth.   2. Cities and towns—
Planning—1945-      3. Zoning.   I. Brower, David J.
HT371.U55           309.2'62            75-19766
ISBN 0-275-55530-5

PRAEGER PUBLISHERS
111 Fourth Avenue, New York, N.Y. 10003, U.S.A.

Published in the United States of America in 1976
by Praeger Publishers, Inc.

Printed in the United States of America

**FOREWORD**
F. Stuart Chapin, Jr.

In the succession of crises that has beset American cities during
the 1960s and 1970s, many involve land use: among them are civil
disorders, environmental pollution, and energy shortages. Civil dis-
turbances can be traced in part to spatial distortions in urban settle-
ment patterns—disparities in access to employment centers, housing,
transportation, and community facilities. It is widely recognized that
such patterns to a significant extent are the result of economic and
minority exclusionary practices in both the public and private sectors,
legitimatized by zoning regulations and building codes, mortgage guarantee policies, and public investment decisions in expressway and rapid rail systems, urban renewal and community infrastructure.

The environmental crisis also has strong land use overtones.
The impact of urbanization on the functioning of natural systems and
the effects on man of the interruption and destruction of the self-
sustaining chain are now widely recognized as progenitors of environmental problems, and hence of environmental protection guidelines.
Increasingly these guidelines place an emphasis on the control of
"nonpoint sources" of pollution, a phrase which has become synono-
mous with land use. On the heels of the environmental crisis, and
certainly not independent of it, is the realization that growth has energy consequences. But the unmonitored element that has slipped into
the American consciousness is the disproportionate rise in energy
consumption in comparison with the acceleration in economic and
population growth. So, in the search for ways of reducing energy consumption, land use again becomes a key pressure point for action, and
the control over density and over inefficient scatter patterns of land
development becomes a part of the solution.

While most observers concede that solutions to such crises involve a number of coordinated actions that encompass a great many
interconnected root causes, a growing emphasis is being placed on the
control of land development as a necessary part of these solutions.
This has come to be known as growth management. As a publicly directed control system, growth management orchestrates a variety of
controls designed to achieve specified growth objectives. The exact
mix of controls, and the weights assigned to their objectives will obviously vary with every metropolitan area, depending on local conditions under pressures of growth, on the extent of impact on various
segments of the population and on interest groups, and on the political
response.

v

A variety of control devices are employed in growth management systems—some regulatory in nature, some involving public investments, and some of a policy nature, namely, the establishment of decision guides for governments to use as a basis for consistency of action. These devices are most effective when conceived and executed jointly in two realms—one having to do with location and the other, with timing. The latter has come to be known as development timing. Of the two, the management of location decisions is more widely understood and used—witness the general acceptance among local officials of such control devices as the land development plan, the capital improvements program, zoning, subdivision control, and the official map. Less understood and less effectively used, at least until relatively recently, is the other realm of growth management, development timing.

This volume therefore has great significance because of the way in which it brings together recent experience in development timing, and analyzes this experience as a part of a growth management strategy. Since the courts have had a profound influence on legislative initiatives in dealing with urban crises—in some respects reversing the traditional roles of legislature and judiciary in pushing for innovation—this volume makes a particularly important contribution in its documentation of court decisions on development timing.

The team which prepared this volume is well-suited to carry out its task. In his leadership of the study, David J. Brower, Director of Urban Services at the Center for Urban and Regional Studies at the University of North Carolina at Chapel Hill, brought a rich background in planning and law to his work. As the catalyst, he gave momentum to the individual contributions of David W. Owens, Ronald Rosenberg, Ira Botvinick and Michael Mandel, all of whom were, when the study was made, advanced students in the University's joint degree program in planning and law.

Many people have made important contributions to this study. Some, including those planners and public officials who took the time to respond to our questionnaire, remain anonymous but nonetheless were essential to the comprehensiveness of the study. The contributions of my coauthors extend beyond the specific pages that they wrote. My associates were valuable advisors at every stage of the project; their stimulation and critical thinking were a constant goad, prodding me to go beyond mere reporting of what is, and to look for the why, for what could be, and for what should be. In this respect, David Owens deserves special mention. Besides cheerfully and efficiently completing the many small jobs that go along with a publication, Dave shared many hours with me discussing the development of and adherence to the purposes of the project. If the quality of these students' work is a true indication, and I believe it is, the outlook for planning and for law is considerably brightened by the prospect of them and others like them entering the two professions.

I also want to give special thanks to Ronald Scott and Paul Brooks of the North Carolina Office of State Planning, who gave invaluable insight and assistance to the project; to Lou Ann Brower, who edited much of the manuscript; to Dianne Teague, who transformed our scribbles into print; to Carroll Carrozza, who tried valiantly to keep the project solvent; and to William Clark, Lydia Kowalski, and Donald Niehus, who did field work in various parts of the country.

Page

ix

## LIST OF TABLES

# Urban Growth Management Through Development Timing

# 1

## INTRODUCTION

Many observers of the American scene are heralding a new mood—Americans are questioning whether growth and development really are desirable objectives.[1] The question of whether to grow or not to grow is appearing on more and more agendas. It is playing a large role in many elections; it has been the subject of an increasing amount of litigation in both federal and state courts. The indications are that the protagonists on each side are just warming to the debate.

"No growth" may be an option, indeed a necessity, for some very special areas facing a very special set of circumstances. But for most jurisdictions no growth is probably not an option. Even though birth rates are declining and the United States may eventually attain zero population growth, there is every indication that our total population will continue to increase for some time to come. There are now so many women of childbearing age and so many women who will soon be reaching childbearing age that the birth rate would have to remain at the zero population growth level for approximately 75 years before population growth would actually stop. In addition, continuing medical advances will extend the average life expectancy, and save the lives of infants and others who now face early death, thus further increasing population levels.

This fact alone has obvious implications for the use of land and for future pressures on urban areas. In addition, our changing life styles work to exacerbate the impact of population growth. The number of households in America is increasing faster than the number of people, and increased demands for housing and land will follow. One indicator of this change is the average size of households in America, a number that has been steadily declining: in 1950 there were 3.4 persons in each household; in 1960 there were 3.3; in 1970 there were 3.2; and in 1972 there were 3.1.[2] Meanwhile the population continued to increase.

TABLE 1

United States Population by Place of Residence

|                          | Percent of Total Population | | |
|                          | 1950 | 1960 | 1970 |
|--------------------------|------|------|------|
| Metropolitan areas       | 62.5 | 66.7 | 68.6 |
| Inside central cities    | 35.5 | 33.5 | 31.4 |
| Outside central cities   | 27.0 | 33.2 | 37.2 |
| Non-metropolitan areas   | 37.5 | 33.3 | 31.4 |

Source: U.S. Bureau of the Census.


It is also clear that much of the growth that will take place will
occur in urban areas. Not only are the newborn more likely than ever
to be urban dwellers, as Table 1 shows, people also are moving from
rural areas to the cities, and from the central city to the suburbs, thus
exerting further pressure on urban areas. By the year 2000 the Census
Bureau expects that five-sixths of the population will be living in urban
areas, and that these areas will occupy about one-sixth of the land area
of the continental United States.

It has been well documented that the growth that has taken place
in this country has not satisfied the spiritual needs of man. This feeling has been confirmed by a number of major studies made by presidential commissions, by many of the states, and by private groups as
well. The reports make the same basic point: we may have more
money than we have ever had, we may have at our disposal more material goods than ever before, but a deeply satisfying life is somehow
beyond our grasp. The quality of life for most Americans does not
meet the high level we have come to expect in our society.

Given that we must grow in the immediate future, we must face
the fact that unbridled, unmanaged growth creates new problems and
leaves the old ones unresolved. Unrestrained, uninhibited, piecemeal
development of land is costly in terms of the consumption of natural
resources, in terms of the demands placed upon government for extended, inefficient service patterns,[3] and in a less specific but perhaps
more significant sense, in terms of the deterioration of the general
quality of life. Life is less pleasant, more burdensome and more expensive in a confused, cluttered atmosphere. There is less public
time and money available for meaningful public services like education, health, and welfare, when so much is consumed in servicing

unmanaged development. There is less private time for meaningful
human activity as individuals are forced to spend inordinate amounts
of time and energy meeting their basic needs in inefficient and wasteful development patterns.

Unmanaged growth has been the pattern. Since growth is inevitable, we must deal with it. If we continue to tolerate the nonmanage-
ment of growth, the consequences, which will multiply, are well known
to all of us.

In a real sense, however, there is no unmanaged growth. Cities
do not simply grow out of thin air. Cities do not naturally sprawl, as
water naturally runs downhill. Buildings are built by men guided by
a series or system of decisions. Urban areas, collections of buildings
and functions grow, blossom, sprawl, thrive, stifle, and die. Cities
do not arise on their own, nor usually because of one man acting alone.
But the entire complex of what we recognize as a city did come about
because of decisions of man. Decisions have been made about the kind
of development that will take place, where it will take place, when it
will take place, and about who will live and work in the area being developed. Those decisions are reflected in the city's form and ability
to function. But the crucial factors of overall goals and coordination
do not have to be present for this sort of managed growth to take place.

We assume in this study that growth will continue to be managed
in the above sense. We raise the issues of who will manage it in the
future and for whose benefit it will be managed.

We assume that growth management will continue to be shared
by the public and private sectors. But we believe that the public role
will grow, and that government may assume a leadership role. This
report also assumes that the public will develop a set of well-articu-
lated objectives, that the questions of where, when, and how we are to
grow will be answered. Thus the study's focus is on the quality of
growth rather than the quantity of growth. Attempts to control the
location, timing, and design of development are based on a wide variety of objectives and imply changing concepts of land, private property, and governmental planning. Controls imposed to achieve these
growth goals depend on the existence of a plan; we have assumed the
existence of a specific, precise plan, which conveys a clear picture
of the future on which both public and private decision makers can
reasonably base their decisions.

The timing of development is of course just one aspect of
managed growth. Timed development, as the term implies, deals
only with the question of when development or growth is going to
occur. What is going to occur, where it is going to occur, and how
much of it will occur will not be covered in this study.

Comprehensive planning is by no means universal. Thus our
assumptions are crucial when applying the tools described here. Our

underlying assumption—which emerges at almost every juncture in
this report—is worth repeating: growth must be managed through the
formulation of goals and objectives. Timed development is only one
tool, the possibilities of which have not yet been fully explored, that
can be used in making a comprehensive plan work.

For some time, planners and public policy makers have recognized the potential for using public investment decisions to affect
growth, and have consequently realized the need for a comprehensive
development strategy based on these investments. However, a public
investment strategy—one type of timed development tool—cannot prevent growth in areas subject to intense development pressures, which
are not, from the public viewpoint, yet suited for development. Nor
has it been highly successful in inducing significant amounts of growth
in areas shunned by private capital. In short, public investment has
been forced to follow private investment, rather than the other way
around. Similarly, the use of isolated, largely negative regulations
and controls has proven ineffective in growth management. Therefore,
it seems that effective growth management requires the coordinated
use of public investment policy, tax policy, and a number of guidance
tools and techniques. This—the idea of the use and coordination of
multiple tools—is the second underlying assumption in this study.
While individual techniques of timed development are presented sepa-
rately, the reader is urged to consider them always in their coordinated use. A managed growth strategy designed to prevent premature
growth and overdevelopment and based on the timing of development
to conserve scarce public funds while protecting valuable natural resources, can potentially stem and channel the rampant growth that
now threatens the quality of our lives.

Our study looks first at constraints that are imposed by the legal system, primarily by the Constitution of the United States, on the
power of a unit of government to time the development of land within
its jurisdiction. We then describe and analyze a number of legal tools
and techniques which are being used in this country to time development. The report then summarizes the responses to a questionnaire
submitted to a number of planning agencies across the country which
were known to have used some form of timed development ordinance
in their managed growth programs. Our conclusions reemphasize the
finding that, while timing is or should be a critical element in any
managed growth system, the existence of a well thought out, well documented, precise, and comprehensive plan is absolutely essential to
any attempt to time development; that most timed development techniques suffer when used by a unit of government whose legal power
to manage growth does not coincide with the geographic area affected
by growth; and finally, that the choice of a specific tool or technique
is not as crucial to its success or failure as is the way in which it is

used, the recognition of both its strengths and its limitations, and the effective coordination of it with other control devices and with the comprehensive plan itself.

## NOTES

1. See, e.g., R. Scott, D. Brower, and D. Miner, eds., Management & Control of Growth: Issues, Techniques, Problems, Trends, 1: 37-111 (1975).

2. U.S. Bureau of the Census, Pocket Data Book, 53 (1973).

3. See generally, Real Estate Research Corporation, The Costs of Sprawl (1974).

# 2

## CONSTITUTIONAL
## CONSTRAINTS ON
## GROWTH MANAGEMENT

All governmental efforts to manage growth through the timing of development must conform to established constitutional limitations on governmental regulation of private action. These constitutional provisions establish the framework within which development timing strategies must be designed. The courts can declare any program which goes beyond these bounds unconstitutional, and thus invalid and unenforceable. If, for example, in an effort to control the timing of development, the government imposes a regulation which restricts the rights of landowners to develop their land and does not compensate them for real or potential financial losses, the courts can determine that the land has been constructively taken for public use and that the regulation is therefore invalid. Thus, any development timing strategy must fall within this and other constitutional limitations on governmental action. An understanding of the constitutional constraints on growth management is a vital prerequisite to the design of any system of development timing.

The basic source of these constraints is the United States Constitution, particularly the Fifth and Fourteenth Amendments. These provisions, as they have been interpreted by the courts, prohibit any unit of government, federal, state, or local, from taking any action which appropriates private land for public use without the payment of compensation, or which unfairly discriminates between similarly situated persons. Furthermore, the courts have also found that necessarily implied in the Constitution is the right to move about freely and settle in any place, even though no such "right to travel" is explicitly set forth.[1]

The constitutions of every state contain statements of rights roughly analogous to the federal Bill of Rights.[2] In many cases, the wording of these provisions is taken directly from the Bill of Rights.[3] Therefore, protection against the violation of these rights can, in many cases, be obtained under either state or federal law.

For example, in the North Carolina state constitution, Article 1, Section 19 provides that "no person shall be taken, imprisoned, or disseized of his freehold, liberties, or privileges, or outlawed, or exiled, or in any manner deprived of his life, liberty, or property, but by law of the land. No person shall be denied the equal protection of the law."

Although this provision does not specifically prohibit the taking of private property for public use without compensation, as is the case with most state constitutions, the courts have long held this prohibition to be necessarily included within it. The North Carolina Supreme Court has said that "the principle is so grounded in natural equity, that it has never been denied to be a part of the law of North Carolina."[4] So, while it is not expressly stated, the North Carolina Constitution has been held to prohibit the taking of private property for public use without the payment of just compensation.[5]

Equal protection clauses of state constitutions, although infrequently litigated in state courts, have been construed to impose the same limitations as the comparable federal provision. It clearly prohibits any arbitrary discrimination.[6]

A similar situation exists with the right to travel. For example, in a recent case involving a city-wide curfew in Asheville, the North Carolina Supreme Court recognized that Article 1, Section 19 of the state constitution also protects the right to travel.[7] However, the court said that the right to travel was not an absolute right—it may be reasonably regulated when necessary to protect the public health and safety.[8] It may be assumed that any growth management strategy in North Carolina which impinges upon the right of individuals to travel freely, which almost all strategies do, will be invalidated unless the court finds it to impose restrictions that are reasonable, and necessary to protect the public health and safety.

The basic purpose of these constitutional provisions is to protect the individual citizen from unreasonable governmental interference; thus they have a direct relevance to governmental attempts to manage growth. Planners and governmental officials must understand the impact that these issues will have on development timing efforts.

These constitutional constraints on growth management must be considered when development timing strategies are being devised. They will affect the choice of tools and techniques to be applied, the balance between direct and indirect controls over the development process, and the application and administration of the programs in specific settings.

This chapter is designed to present some of the basic information necessary for the development of an understanding of the impact these constitutional constraints will have on growth management. Without this understanding, those designing development timing strategies face a dual risk: first, strategies may be developed which will not be given legal effect because they overstep constitutional bounds; second, and perhaps more importantly, more effective development timing strategies may not even be attempted because of unfounded fears of unconstitutionality.9 Because the law in this area is still developing, firm conclusions on the exact constitutional bounds to growth management cannot be provided by this or any other report. Still, it is possible to provide the information necessary for thoughtful consideration of these complex issues; this chapter will do so.

## THE TAKING ISSUE

The "taking issue" is one of the most controversial judicial issues to arise in recent times. The number of landmark cases decided since the early 1960s alone reveals the importance and pervasiveness of the problem.

The taking issue grows out of the Fifth Amendment to the Constitution of the United States, which reads, in part, ". . . nor shall any person . . . be deprived of life, liberty, or property, without due process of law; nor shall private property be taken for public use without just compensation."10 A judicial decision that a government, by whatever means, has so acted as to "take" private property for public use requires that compensation be paid to the landowner. A regulation which completely restricts or substantially impairs the property of a landowner (in circumstances that will be discussed later) so as to render the property "taken" is unconstitutional unless compensation is paid to the property owner.

This safeguard has its source in the English system of jurisprudence. The Magna Carta, signed more than five hundred years before the American Constitution was conceived, stated that "no freeman shall be arrested, or detained in prison, or deprived of his freehold, or in any way molested; and we will not set forth against him, nor send against, unless by the lawful judgment of his peers and by the law of the land."11 (Emphasis added) It is not surprising that our Founding Fathers would provide similar provisions in their own charter.

Sir William Blackstone, a noted legal commentator on British legal tradition, wrote:

> So great moreover is the regard of the law for private property, that it will not authorize the least violation of it; no, not even for the general good of the whole community. If a new road, for instance, were to be made

through the grounds of a private person, it might perhaps
be extensively beneficial to the public; but the law permits
no man, or set of men, to do this without consent of the
owner of the land. <u>In vain may it be urged, that the good</u>
<u>of the individual ought to yield to that of the community;</u>
<u>for it would be dangerous to allow any private man, or</u>
<u>even any public tribunal, to be the judge of the common</u>
<u>good, and to decide whether it be expedient or no.</u> Be-
sides, the public good is in nothing more essentially interested, than in the protection of every individual's
private rights, as modeled by the municipal law.[12]
(Emphasis added.)

However, Blackstone's dogmatic view of the sacredness of one's
property must be tempered by another feature of common law which
the American judicial system has adopted: the law of nuisance.
Through the years the courts have constrained property owners from
exercising free reign on their property. Such activities as operation
of a cement plant in certain areas;[13] operating a piggery in a residential community;[14] or maintaining feed grinding and feed mixing
facilities and selling fertilizer[15] have been declared nuisances, and
courts have either granted injunctions or have required damage payments from the offenders.

Basically, "nuisance" is defined as any "activity, occupation,
or structure" which "impairs the health, safety, morals, or welfare
of the general community," or "unreasonably interferes with the use
and enjoyment of another's land."[16] The courts tend to stress the
importance of the right of a landowner to enjoy the use of his property,
but not at the expense of an adjoining landowner, or the public in general.

Government restricts property in another way. Since the 1920s,
the courts have sanctioned zoning, which certainly limits—in some
cases almost entirely destroys—the value of certain property and the
rights of a given landowner.[17] Why? Underlying court decisions in
this area is the idea that the individual is, in certain cases, best
served by public regulation of property rights.

In dealing with the taking issue, we are not merely talking about
the appropriation of one's land by government. There is a more cumbersome problem:

When a social decision to redirect economic resources
entails painfully obvious opportunity costs, how shall these
costs ultimately be distributed among all the members
of society? Shall they be permitted to remain where they
fall initially or shall the government, by paying

> compensation, make explicit attempts to distribute them
> in accordance with decisions made by whatever process
> fashions the tax structure, or perhaps according to some
> other principle? Shall the losses be left with the individ-
> uals on whom they happen first to fall, or shall they be
> "socialized?"[18]

Government regulation often results in windfall profits or "wipe-out"
losses, and the question becomes, who will bear the consequences of
governmental decisions? The question has been deliberated for almost
two hundred years with no definitive conclusions.

### Different Approaches to the Taking Issue

The taking issue has had a curious history in the United States.
Understandably, there was little litigation during the early history of
the country, because there was so much land available for any imagi-
nable use.

#### Positive Encroachment versus Negative Restriction

One of the first Supreme Court cases on the taking issue was
Pumpelly v. Green Bay Co., which held that a landowner's property
had indeed been taken when it had been flooded under a regulation
calling for flood control and construction of dams.[19] The Court felt
a potential inequity would arise

> if . . . it shall be held that if the government refrains
> from the absolute conversion of real property to the uses
> of the public it can destroy the value entirely; can inflict
> irreparable and permanent injury to any extent; can, in
> effect, subject it to total destruction without making any
> compensation, because in the narrow sense of the word,
> it is not taken for public use.[20]

However, in Transportation Co. v. Chicago,[21] the Court denied compensation to a landowner whose property had been damaged during
construction of a tunnel under the Chicago River, holding that the decision in Pumpelly was limited to direct encroachments of a permanent nature.

> Acts done in the proper exercise of governmental powers,
> and not directly encroaching upon private property, though

their consequences may impair its use, are universally
held not to be a taking within the meaning of the constitutional provision.[22]

These first cases established the first legal concept of taking, dis-
tinguishing positive encroachment from negative restriction or indirect, consequential damages. While encroachment may be given the
same weight as a forced, physical taking, the encroachment must be
permanent. Moreover, the consequential damages from indirect encroachments were not considered takings, insofar as taking might require compensation.

## Prohibition of Harmful Activity versus Benefit to the Public

The Government enjoyed the interpretation set forth by Pumpelly
and Transportation Co. for some time; and its legal position was bol-
stered by another landmark decision, Mugler v. Kansas.[23] There, the
state had forbidden the sale and manufacture of intoxicating liquids.
The claimant argued that since his breweries had been erected for
purposes that had been legal at the time, a regulation that destroyed
their economic value could not be enforced without compensation for
the loss of value to the property. The court held that there was no
taking because there was no ''appropriation of property for the public
benefit but merely a limitation upon use by the owner for certain purposes declared to be injurous to the community.''[24] As Mr. Justice
Brandeis wrote:

> The property so restricted remains in the possession of
> its owner. The State does not appropriate it or make a
> use of it which interferes with paramount rights to the
> public. The State merely prevents the owner from making
> a use which interferes with paramount rights to the pub-
> lic. Whenever the use prohibited ceases to be noxious,—
> as it may because of further changes in local or social
> conditions,—the restriction will have to be removed and
> the owner will again be free to enjoy his property as
> heretofore.[25]

It is interesting to note that in the particular case, the brewery had
been a long-standing structure, and for all practical purposes the
land was indeed worthless if it could not be used for its original purpose. At the very least, it would have taken substantial sums to con-
vert the property to profitable activities. Yet the Court held that no
taking had occurred.

This second theory associated with the taking issue may be stated as follows: "Does the restriction prohibit harmful activity or does it actively benefit the public?" In the first instance compensation would be denied; in the second, compensation would be paid. The government should not be allowed to take a property owner's windfall gains, but at the same time it should not have to pay compensation because a regulation prohibited a use of land that is not in the public interest.

A recent case, Just v. Marinette Co., follows this general theory.[26] In the Just case, a Wisconsin county adopted an ordinance which included a provision prohibiting filling of more than five hundred square feet of wetlands contiguous to navigable waters without a special permit. The Wisconsin Supreme Court upheld a lower court's decision that the ordinance reflected a constitutional exercise of the state's police power. It approached the problem by applying a test for compensation based on a distinction between restrictions "placed on property to restrain conduct harmful to the public and those designed to secure a benefit not presently enjoyed by the public."[27] The latter instance would require compensation for any diminution in value caused to the property. Under the particular facts, the court held that the regulation prevented a harm, and thus did not constitute a taking of petitioner's property. The court said that "an owner of land has no absolute and unlimited right to change the essential character of his land so as to use it for a purpose for which it was unsuited in its natural state and which injures the rights of others."[28] The Just case thus reiterates what Justice Brandeis had written almost one hundred years before. In this case, like the brewery example cited above, the landowner was allowed to suffer substantial economic losses without being compensated.

## Diminution in Value

Justice Oliver Wendell Holmes had different views on the taking issue.[29] Justice Holmes's approach is most commonly referred to as the "diminution in value" theory; he evaluated the degree of economic harm a landowner suffered from a government regulation. His position is best reflected in the landmark decision, Pennsylvania Coal Co. v. Mahon.[30] A statute prohibited mining practices that would remove support and cause subsidence of houses built over the mines. The Court held the statute to be an unconstitutional taking. The statute would destroy the mining right which the coal company had retained when it first sold the property. Justice Holmes wrote:

One fact for consideration . . . is the extent of the diminution. When it reaches a certain magnitude, in most if

not all cases there must be an exercise of eminent domain
and compensation to sustain the act. . . . The general rule,
at least, is that while property may be regulated to a certain extent, if regulation goes too far it will be recognized
as a taking.[31]

It is interesting to note that an equally famous statement—one which
is frequently quoted when cases involving the taking issue arise today—
is from the dissenting opinion in the same case, by Justice Brandeis:

Every restriction upon the use of property, imposed in the
exercise of the police power, deprives the owner of some
right theretofore enjoyed, and is, in that sense, an abridge-
ment by the state of rights and properties without making
compensation. But restriction imposed to protect the public health, safety, or morals from dangers threatened is
not a taking. The restriction here in question is merely the
prohibition of a noxious use.[32]

Forty years later, the Court again was faced with a situation
involving an alleged taking in the municipal regulation of land use.
In Goldblatt v. Town of Hempstead, the city sought injunctive relief
against a landowner who continued mining operations, in disregard of
a municipal ordinance prohibiting mining operations below the water
table. Under the circumstances of the case, to comply with the ordinance would have resulted in the owner's ceasing completely all mining operations. Nevertheless, the Supreme Court upheld the validity
of the ordinance on the grounds that it was a reasonable exercise of
the police power.[33]

Though the city sought to uphold the ordinance as a safety measure, the Court looked at many of its other implications, including the
diminution in value it caused and other uses of the property that may
have been possible. Underlying this investigation was the assumption
that the landowner had the burden of proving the unreasonableness of
the ordinance. Since the landowner had not shown that there were no
other feasible alternatives for utilizing the property, the ordinance
could not be invalidated.

While the decision of Justice Holmes in Pennsylvania Coal may
seem excessively stringent, it has been the prevailing view. Many
cases followed a strict interpretation of taking and allowed extensive
regulation.[34] One decision even held that near-total destruction of
property might be permitted without compensation.[35] The diminution
in value analysis is a viable judicial tool, and is often seen today in
the resolution of cases involving the taking issue.

The Balancing Theory

The last major approach to the taking issue is called the "balancing theory," and is best characterized by the phrase "balancing the good to be gained from the regulation as opposed to the extent of private loss." It was derived from the Pennsylvania Coal case, perhaps inferred from the general rule stated by Holmes even though his opinion employed no balancing test as such, but instead called the regulation invalid because the mining rights were destroyed.

This approach allows government a great deal of latitude but is not legally sound. The language of the Fifth Amendment is clear: ". . . nor shall property be taken for public use, without just compensation." (Emphasis added.) The issue is not how great the public benefit is, but whether property was taken. If property was taken, then compensation must be made. Like the direct encroachment theory and the prohibition of harmful activity theory, the balancing theory can have very disastrous results for the landowner, whatever harm he may have caused. "If the extent of private loss [is] of less weight than the magnitude of public need embodied in the challenged governmental action," compensation could be denied.36 In spite of its lack of constitutional basis, a number of courts recognize this test as sound rationale.

Even though four seemingly distinctive tests have been set forth here, it should be clear that application of any one of them will not predict whether an award or denial of compensation will be made in a particular case. Perhaps the most accurate way of describing judicial activity in this area is to say that whether or not there is a taking in a given situation depends on the facts of the particular case, with the judges hoping to arrive at an equitable result. Unfortunately, the equitable result is not always found.


Implications of the Taking Issue


No one should question the far-reaching impact of the decisions related to the taking issue. They affect many important planning considerations. A few are highlighted below.

Subdivision Regulation

Historically, local governments have put constraints on a landowner's ability to divide a parcel of land into a number of smaller parcels. Such subdivision regulations have been upheld on a variety of legal theories, some of which do not stand up on close examination.37

Under the "voluntary act theory," since no one forces a landowner to divide his land, he should be required to meet certain exactions set forth by the locality if he does so. Another equally unsound doctrine is called the "privilege theory." Its reasoning is as follows: the locality, through enabling legislation from the state, allows the landowner to subdivide, but is under no obligation to do so; and therefore, the landowner should have to pay for the privilege of subdividing. "Payment" is defined as meeting the required exactions. The third theory, the "police power theory," is more sound legally; according to it, the locality, in seeking to protect the health, safety, and welfare of the community, is clearly within its powers to require exactions.

The most common requirement found in subdivision regulations is the necessity for dedicating land in the subdivision for streets and utilities. Less frequent, but certainly the trend which newer regulations incorporate, is the requirement that land be dedicated for school sites, parks, or other public places,[38] or that a payment be made in lieu of dedicating the land.[39] It is also fairly common to find a number of the following amenities required to be provided by subdivision regulations.[40]

| | |
|---|---|
| curbs and gutters | sewers |
| storm drains | street lights |
| fire alarm systems | water mains |
| gas lines | planting strips |
| telephone systems | bridges and/or fences |

Although generally the amenities that developers have been required to provide were declared to be primarily for the benefit of the people who actually live in the subdivision, in Jenad, Inc. v. Village of Scarsdale, the court upheld a requirement that the developer either dedicate land for recreational purposes or pay an in-lieu fee, regardless of whom the park would primarily benefit.[41] However, courts have not always upheld the localities' right to impose subdivision regulations. The court in East Neck Estates, Ltd. v. Luchsinger held unconstitutional an exaction which required a developer to dedicate a strip of land which amounted to almost one-third of the total value of the property.[42] Generally, however, local governments and their planning agencies are given a great deal of flexibility with subdivision regulation.

Wetlands Regulation

While the courts are not easily dissuaded from a judicial position which embraces the idea of well-established property rights—most importantly, the right of a property owner to receive a return

from his land—they have become increasingly willing to uphold government regulation on the theory that the public is being protected
from actual or even potential harm.[43] Unfortunately, there is no uniformity to these decisions, and similar fact situations have been decided differently. A number of decisions have invalidated certain land
use plans relating to wetlands.[44] The courts noted the importance of
wetlands preservation, and the public interest that is served, but
felt that these factors were outweighed by the severe diminution of
property value which left the landowner without reasonable alternatives.

One of the best-known contrary decisions in this area is Candle-
stick Properties, Inc. v. San Francisco Bay Conservation and Development Commission.[45] In that case, impressed by strong legislative
reports as to calamitous effects to the environment that might be
caused by filling the San Francisco Bay, the court upheld a directive
of the San Francisco Bay Conservation and Development Commission
which prohibited filling of the Bay. Arguing that the intent of the directive was to prevent harm, the court held that the commission had
grounds for regulation and that compensation was not required:

> . . . the police power, as such, is not confined within the
> narrow circumspection of precedents, resting upon past
> conditions which do not cover and control present day con-
> ditions . . . that is to say, as a commonwealth develops
> politically, economically, and socially, the police power
> likewise develops, within reason, to meet the changing
> conditions.[46]

An undercurrent of change is clearly developing, and legislative findings of ecological harm have been used as judicial justification for upholding a statute which otherwise greatly diminished the value of
private property. A strict diminution in value test may no longer be
strictly applied to cases of this kind.

## Timing Development

Timing development in a municipality is a relatively new tool,
and one which has of late been exposed to rather critical attack.[47]
Challenge on the grounds of taking is a cumbersome judicial undertaking and, in fact, failed in Golden v. Planning Board of the Town
of Ramapo.[48]

In the Ramapo case, the municipality involved adopted a program that would allow for staggered growth, in accordance with a
capital investment program providing for an extension of municipal
services. Suit was filed by a developer desiring to construct apart-

ments for middle- and upper-income families. Among the issues raised was whether, by denying the owner the right to develop for up to eighteen years, the ordinances represented an unconstitutional taking of private land. The trial court ruled that the regulation was indeed valid because of the remedies available to the landowner, and also because the restrictions were neither permanent nor unreasonable. The appellate court did not deal directly with the taking issue, but a concurring opinion stated that a governmental ''freeze'' on residential development for a ''lengthy duration'' might be considered arbitrary and unreasonable and therefore constitute a taking without compensation. The question here is, ''How long is too long?'' We know from the opinion that eighteen years is not to be considered excessive.

The Ramapo case shows that courts have been willing to go beyond the traditional limits of the taking clause and to provide a certain amount of flexibility to government when a regulation reflects careful study and expert consideration, as the Ramapo plan did. The precedent has been set, the initial step has been taken, and the limits of the taking clause cannot be considered as narrowly defined as they once were.

## Zoning: General

The taking issue is certainly relevant to a discussion of zoning. In Consolidated Rock Products Co. v. City of Los Angeles, the plaintiff's land, which was basically suited only to gravel pit operations, was restricted to agricultural and residential uses, in accordance with a comprehensive plan for the City of Los Angeles. Even though the property had been devalued to virtually nothing, the trial court held, and the California Supreme Court affirmed, that the restriction was a valid exercise of the police power.[49] The California rule on judicial review has been summarized as ''. . . when reasonable minds differ on the relation of a zoning ordinance to the police power goals of health, safety, morals, or the general welfare, the court will not substitute its judgment for that of the legislature.''[50]

The legal arguments in defense of zoning have relied on this point in many cases. For this reason, localities must be prepared to show the relationship of a particular ordinance to police power objectives.

## Zoning: Large Lot

Large lot zoning is a relatively new tool for managing growth. For example, Santa Cruz County has established 40-acre minimums on certain portions of its land; its regulation is currently under attack

as an unconstitutional taking.[51] The City of Palo Alto adopted open
space regulations, and the owner of a sizable tract of land is attacking
the provision on similar grounds.[52]

Two cases seem to give some insight into the position of the
courts on the issue of large lot zoning. The court in Steel Hill Development, Inc. v. Town of Sanbornton[53] upheld an ordinance which required three-acre and six-acre minimum lots in certain zones. The
court noted that such ordinances must be within the purview of established police power purposes—health, safety, welfare, and morals—
and that the ordinance in question was. The ordinance was upheld,
despite the fact that the court was "disturbed by the admission here
that there was never any professional or scientific study made as to
why six, rather than four or eight acres was reasonable to protect
values cherished."[54] While the outcome of this case was favorable
to government, it is obvious that planners could have made a valuable
contribution towards strengthening it. In fact, it may be crucial for
planners to be utilized more frequently when ordinances concerning
land use are being prepared. Other courts may not as easily overlook
the lack of scientific surveys underlying local ordinances as the Steel
Hill court did.

The other case, which held a zoning ordinance with four-acre
minimum lots invalid, offers further insights into the problem. The
court in National Land & Investment Co. v. Easttown Township Board
of Adjustment noted that "there is no doubt that . . . zoning for density
is a legitimate exercise of the police power [citations omitted]. . . .
Therefore, it is impossible for us to say that any minimum acreage
requirement is unconstitutional per se."[55] The case was not decided
by the fact that the property would greatly diminish in value (from
more than $250,000 to approximately $175,000). The court found for
the landowners on the basis of the city's failure to show the public
purpose behind the minimum acreage requirements. It appears that
courts will be willing to uphold certain minimum lot size requirements
provided that local governments provide ample proof that the restrictions are environmentally sound.

Conclusions


The taking clause, in and of itself, is no real obstacle to managed growth. Courts have upheld a wide range of regulations, some
of which reach beyond the normal limits of control. What is crucial
to a municipality's successful defense of its proposed regulation is
an accumulation of evidence to support the need for the control. The
most convincing kinds of evidence, in terms of judicial acceptance, are

legislative reports, planning reports, and scientific evidence of ecological and other environmental factors. Without these kinds of support, a governmental defendant has only the uncertain hope that the
courts will liberally apply the precedents on the taking issue. A government is on firmer ground if it shows evidence that the purpose of
the restriction falls within the definition of a valid police power. As
we have seen, courts presented with material of this kind will uphold
stringent regulations.

## EQUAL PROTECTION OF THE LAWS

The Fourteenth Amendment is one of the cornerstones of American justice. Enacted in 1868, largely to assure the constitutional validity of the Civil Rights Act of 1866, the Fourteenth Amendment is the
only provision in the United States Constitution specifically devoted
to assuring equality before the law.

In the early application of the amendment, its original intent of
Equal Protection was diverted to fit the needs of the changing economy
of the late stages of the industrial revolution, and it was directed towards questions of government economic regulation. Later, during the
New Deal the equal protection clause, in conjunction with the due process clause, was used to invalidate early labor legislation.[56] But in
the postwar era, society and the courts, reflecting a general concern
for social justice, have gradually expanded the scope of equal protection to include school desegregation,[57] voter reapportionment,[58]
family law,[59] and criminal procedure.[60] Recently, urban growth activities—the provision of public facilities such as roads, water and
sewer systems,[61] the siting of low-cost public housing projects,[62]
the establishment of zoning ordinances,[63] and the relocation of dis-
placed urban renewal residents[64]—have all been scrutinized for possible denial of equal protection.

Consequently, planners must be aware of the constitutional constraints on the growth management tools that they select to harmo-
nize development and resources. The purposes of this section are to
outline the basic principles of equal protection, to explain what is
meant by equal protection of the laws, to determine when the provision becomes operative, and to understand how the courts apply the
doctrine.

It must be remembered, to begin with, that the equal protection
clause does not require strict equality. Rather, it requires that a
law which intentionally or unintentionally imposes classifications
which treat persons or property differently must be justified by a
permissible government objective. Permissible governmental

objectives include public safety, health, morals, and general welfare. Thus, the equal protection clause allows government to differentiate if it has a valid reason for doing so. To illustrate, differential treatment of similarly located parcels of land can be justified if localities act according to a comprehensive plan that provides a reasonable basis for the differential treatment.[65] Second, when framing the Fourteenth Amendment the Radical Republicans who dominated Congress anticipated interference with the enforcement of reconstruction legislation from recalcitrant southern states, and they drafted the equal protection clause to provide that "no state shall . . . deny to any person within its jurisdiction the equal protection of the law." Thus, the equal protection clause applies only to state action and does not prevent private persons or associations from discriminating.[66] Therefore, before the courts can apply an equal protection standard state action must first be shown.

State Action

The most obvious form of state action is state legislation and activities by state officials, but the term is a comprehensive one that also denotes the activities of local officials, such as police, building code inspectors, and zoning administrators, and the actions of all local agencies operating under the color of law.

The Supreme Court in the landmark case Shelley v. Kraemer held that state action is present whenever the courts give legal sanction to racial discrimination by private parties. Applying this rationale, the Court held that the judicial enforcement of racially restrictive covenants constitutes state action and violates the equal protection clause.[67]

Even presentation of a referendum to voters may constitute illegal state action. For example, in Reitman v. Mulkey, a California referendum repealing the state's fair housing ordinance was declared unconstitutional.[68]

Finally, in two recent cases related to growth management, nonfeasance—failing to act—has constituted state action. In Kennedy Park Homes v. City of Lackawanna, local officials failed to issue building permits,[69] and in United Farmworkers of Florida Housing Project, Inc. v. City of Delray Beach, they refused to permit sewer and water hook-ups.[70] In the two cases, separate federal courts of appeals held that the defendants' conduct constituted state action.

## The Equal Protection Standard

In applying the equal protection clause a two-tier test is used by the courts, consisting of the "rationality test," and "strict scrutiny" analysis.

### The Rationality Test

To decide whether a law violates the equal protection clause, the courts consider three factors: (1) the governmental objective asserted in support of the classification; (2) the character of the classification; and (3) the individual interest affected by the classification. Thus, in defining the constitutional scope of growth management tools, the courts first ask whether the contested regulation is designed to achieve permissible objectives. If it does not, then it will be declared unconstitutional. For example, Fairfax County, Virginia, adopted a two-acre minimum lot zoning classification and placed the western two-thirds of its area under it. Although the ordinance was designed to concentrate growth in the eastern part of the country, it had the practical effect of excluding low-income families from the western part. The Virginia Supreme Court held in Board of County Supervisors of Fairfax County v. Carper, that this result represented an impermissible governmental objective.71

If a permissible objective is present, the courts then analyze the connection between objectives and state action. The rationality test requires that state action be rationally related to permissible objectives. If the relationship lacks a rational basis the regulation will be declared unconstitutional. For example, the city of Cranston, Rhode Island, enacted a subdivision ordinance which required that a fixed percent of the total land being subdivided by developers be dedicated for public schools and open spaces. Although the dedication served a permissible objective, the fixed percent method failed to reflect an actual need. The Rhode Island Supreme Court held in Frank Ansuni, Inc. v. City of Cranston, that the city's requirement for a fixed percent dedication was irrational because it imposed the same burdens on one-acre lots as on multi-family complexes, despite the obviously different needs generated by the two subdivisions.72

With regard to the second factor, the character of the governmental classification, if the classification is applied to maintain racial discrimination, the governmental program is unconstitutional. Applying this rationale, a federal court of appeals invalidated a Lackawanna, New York building permit moratorium, even though the moratorium was justified on the basis of inadequate sewage treatment facilities.73

Lastly, the courts examine the individual interest affected by the classification. If the classification infringes upon fundamental constitutional rights or is based on a suspect classification, the courts apply a strict scrutiny test.

## Strict Scrutiny

While under the rationality test, the courts will be satisfied with proof that a permissible governmental objective is promoted, under a strict scrutiny test, they may invalidate governmental action which interferes with fundamental constitutional rights, unless it is supported by a compelling interest. The Supreme Court has not defined fundamental rights, nor has it established guidelines for determining when interference with these rights occurs. However, in past cases the Supreme Court has indicated that fundamental rights are limited to constitutional rights such as the right to vote,[74] the right to travel,[75] the right to procreate,[76] the right to freedom of expression,[77] and the various rights of criminal defendants.[78] Such necessities of life as welfare payments[79] and housing[80] are not considered fundamental rights. While previous cases indicate that interference with fundamental constitutional rights means substantially less in judicial terms than a complete denial of them, a planner anticipating constitutional adjudication must be aware that the courts will apply a strict scrutiny test if governmental action could possibly impinge on fundamental constitutional rights. For example, the charging of a poll tax may discourage voting,[81] and a one-year welfare residency law may discourage travel;[82] under strict scrutiny, these forms of state action have been held unconstitutional.

The other situation in which the strict scrutiny test is required is when the classifying trait is deemed suspect. Classifications on the basis of race[83] and of national origin[84] have been struck down for this reason.

The application of the strict scrutiny test has three important consequences: First, it shifts the burden of proof from complainant to government. Second, when a strict scrutiny test is applied, government must justify the classification by showing a compelling governmental interest, not merely a permissible objective, to sustain an infringement of fundamental rights. Finally, the courts in a strict scrutiny analysis examine the impact of state action, rather than its intent. Desirable urban planning policies such as providing low-cost public housing to inner-city residents may be declared unconstitutional if their real effect is to perpetuate racially segregated housing.[85]

The following two cases further clarify and illustrate the application of the two-tier equal protection test.

In the first case, the Ohio state legislature passes an ad valorem tax on merchandise stored in Ohio warehouses. The law, however, exampts merchandise belonging to non-Ohio residents. Ohio residents allege that they are being denied equal protection under the law. The court first determines that the Ohio law is related to the permissible governmental objective of stimulating economic growth. It further holds that encouraging nonresidents to locate merchandise in Ohio warehouses is a rational means of carrying out the government's objective, and that therefore the classifying trait is noncapricious; no fundamental constitutional right is impeded. The law is upheld.[86]

In the second case, the city of Newport, Rhode Island passes an ordinance requiring persons to be residents of Newport for at least two years before they are eligible for low-cost public housing. The ordinance is challenged. The court first applies the test of rationality, and determines that granting long-standing resident taxpayers the first opportunity for public housing is related to a permissible objective, community stability. The residency requirement is held to be rationally related to the objective, and as a result the ordinance is found to be applied noncapriciously. However, the durational residency classification impedes the fundamental constitutional right to travel, and so a strict scrutiny test is applied. The court decides that the city's objective of allowing long-standing resident taxpayers the first opportunity for public housing is not of such compelling importance that a basic constitutional right should be threatened. The ordinance is therefore held unconstitutional.[87]

These two examples illustrate two important principles of constitutional adjudication. First, the decision of whether or not the strict scrutiny test must be applied depends not on a court's whim, but on whether fundamental constitutional rights have been denied. Second, the equal protection clause is similarly applied to both state laws and local ordinances.

## Conclusions

Although the law is changing and definitive statements about the constitutionality of recently developed managed growth tools are not possible, previous court pronouncements provide three general guidelines. First, policies which have the effect of continuing racial discrimination will be declared unconstitutional.[88] Second, states and localities are prohibited from choosing means that unnecessarily burden or restrict a constitutionally protected activity.[89] Therefore, the courts are more likely to invalidate an ordinance if there are less restrictive managed growth tools available to achieve comparable government ends.[90]

Finally, although the judicial imperative that land use and community development plans meet the demands of equal protection at first may appear too stringent and too uncertain to allow free use of planning techniques, in actuality, the requirements of equal protection support rather than undermine rational planning efforts. If the technique being challenged is related to a sensible and comprehensive plan, the test of rationality can often be met. And if the plan is developed on the basis of a reasonable geographic area in which the rights of individuals and the needs of all groups are considered, protection of basic rights and avoidance of invidious classification and discrimination will be part of its natural evolution.

## THE RIGHT TO TRAVEL

Unlike due process and equal protection, which have long histories, the right to travel is at the cutting edge of legal thought. Only within the last five years has it been applied to durational residence laws in voting,[91] civil service employment[92] and public housing,[93] out-of-state college tuition fees,[94] and provision of health services.[95] Consequently, while the legal implications of the right to travel for managed growth efforts are uncertain, managed growth will affect mobility and thus will have to face challenges based on interference with the right to travel. Thus when the city of Petaluma, California adopted a city ordinance which limited the number of new housing units to five hundred annually over a five-year period, a United States district court held that this growth limitation restricted the right to travel and declared the ordinance unconstitutional.[96] This case is significant because it is the first case in American jurisprudence in which the right to travel has been applied to managed growth tools. On appeal to the United States Court of Appeals for the Ninth Circuit, the ordinance was upheld, with the court dismissing the right to travel challenge on the grounds that none of the plaintiffs had standing to assert it.[97]

### History of the Right to Travel

Although the right to travel has been extensively cited only within the last decade, it originated in English common law. Article 42 of the Magna Carta allowed every freeman to leave England except during time of war. In this country, Article 4 of the Articles of Confederation provided that ''the people shall have free ingress and regress to and from any other state.''

Although the right to travel is not explicitly mentioned in the Constitution, the courts have long recognized it as a constitutional right. The first judicial recognition of this right occurred in 1823 in Corfield v. Coryell.[98] In that case a federal appellate court characterized the right as one of the fundamental privileges and immunities under Article 1, Section 2 of the Constitution: "The citizens of each state shall be entitled to all privileges and immunities of citizens in the several states." Applying this same rationale the United States Supreme Court forty-five years later in Crandall v. Nevada invalidated a Nevada tax on every person leaving the state by common carrier.[99] This was the first time the United States Supreme Court recognized the right to travel. Since that time, the privileges and immunities clause of the Fourteenth Amendment,[100] the due process clause of the Fifth Amendment,[101] and the commerce clause of Article 1[102] have all been proffered to support the right to travel.

The right to travel, however, did not become a potent doctrine until Aptheker v. Secretary of State.[103] In that case, the Supreme Court found that the right to travel was closely related to First Amendment freedoms. This association is significant because First Amendment rights are accorded special protection.[104] For example, any law which infringes upon First Amendment rights can be challenged without alleging personal injury or unlawful application of the law. Moreover, any infringement on First Amendment rights must be justified by a compelling governmental interest.[105] Furthermore, unlike the equal protection clause, First Amendment rights are secured against interference from both governmental and private sources.[106] Thus by associating the right to travel with First Amendment freedoms, the Court implicitly accorded the right to travel the same special protection granted other First Amendment liberties.

The evolution of "right to travel" from an obscure doctrine subsumed as part of the privileges and immunities clause to a First Amendment right was completed in Shapiro v. Thompson, in which, using the right to travel to invalidate a one-year welfare residency requirement, the Supreme Court made explicit the assumptions made implicit in the Aptheker decision.[107] The Shapiro decision is significant for two reasons: first, it expanded the right to travel to include indirect infringements such as user fees and residency requirements. Before Shapiro previous travel cases had been directly concerned with travel. Second, the court invoked a compelling interest test, and thereby extended to travel the same preferred protection granted to other First Amendment rights.

## The Right to Travel Standard

Although the right to travel is a fundamental constitutional right, it does not follow that travel cannot be regulated. To determine

whether a law violates the right to travel, the courts look to two
things: first, the extent to which travel is interfered with; and second, the governmental interest involved. Therefore, managed growth
tools can be upheld on either of two grounds: first, the regulation
may not substantially interfere with the right to travel; and second,
the regulation may promote a compelling governmental interest.


### The Extent of Interference


To some extent, any managed growth tool may impede the ability
of a person to move his or her place of residence. The courts, however, have held that not all regulations which affect travel are unconstitutional. To illustrate, the University of Minnesota presumes, for
the purpose of determining tuition charges, that all non-Minnesota
students are out-of-state residents for one year, and must pay out-
of-state tuition fees. Despite this policy, nearly one-sixth of the students are nonresidents. Consequently, the court in Starns v. Malkerson held that University policy did not deter out-of-state students
from attending the University of Minnesota.[108] The City of Hermosa
Beach, California enacted an ordinance making it unlawful to rent to
anyone under age 18 without having a responsible adult as a cotenant.
The court, in Ames v. City of Hermosa Beach, held that this ordinance
did not impede mobility.[109]

Previous court opinions have indicated that policies which attempt to fence people out violate the right to travel. For example, in
a case discussed earlier, the two-year residency requirement for public housing eligibility that attempted to discourage indigents from
settling in the City of Newport, Rhode Island was declared unconstitutional.[110] Moreover, the right to travel includes both interstate and
intrastate travel. As the Second Circuit Court of Appeals has stated,
"It would be meaningless to describe the right to travel between states
as a fundamental precept of personal liberty and not acknowledge a
correlative constitutional right to travel within a state."[111]


### Compelling State Interest


Even in those situations where the right to travel has been restricted, the courts will uphold the restriction if the government can
show a compelling interest for it. The courts have not defined compelling interest, but they have named some of the interests that are

not compelling. The Supreme Court in Shapiro v. Thompson[112] held that maintaining fiscal integrity of the state welfare program,[113] detering indigents from entering that state,[114] maintaining administrative efficiency,[115] and limiting the welfare burden on taxpayers were not compelling state interests.[116]

In previous cases the Supreme Court has indicated that exigent circumstances are a compelling interest. The Court has also stated: "(A)reas ravaged by flood, fire or epidemic can be quarantined when it can be demonstrated that unlimited travel would jeopardize the safety and welfare of the area or the nation as a whole."[117] This rationale has been used to uphold city-wide curfews.[118] Moreover, exigent environmental circumstances could also justify a restriction on the right to travel.

Compelling government interests other than exigent ones have been upheld. In Kezewinski v. Kugler, a New Jersey statute which required policemen and firemen to be residents in the municipality where they were employed was justified by the compelling state interest of promoting law enforcement.[119]

## Conclusion

The right to travel may have important legal implications for managed growth. Managed growth tools which seriously restrict mobility are likely to be challenged. However, it should also be recognized that the right to travel, like other constitutional principles, is subject to limitations.

If managing growth in individual cases can be shown to be a compelling governmental interest, then even those managed growth tools which infringe upon the right to travel can be sustained. Consequently, the right to travel should not seriously constrain well-designed managed growth programs. However, in the light of what has been discussed above, planners may be required to (1) assess the impact of managed growth efforts in terms of travel, and (2) attempt to select tools which minimize interference with the right to travel.

## NOTES

1. The Supreme Court has long recognized that the freedom to travel, which includes the right to migrate and settle in any state or

municipality, is a fundamental right protected by the U.S. Constitution.
See, e.g., Memorial Hospital v. Maricopa County, 415 U.S. 250 (1974);
Dunn v. Blumstein, 405 U.S. 330 (1972); Shapiro v. Thompson 394 U.S.
618 (1969); Edwards v. California, 314 U.S. 160 (1941).

2. See Legislative Drafting Research Fund, Columbia University,
Constitutions of the United States, National and State (Supp. 1969).

3. For the "takings" clauses, see, e.g., Cal. Const. Art. 1, § 14;
N.Y. Const. Art. 1, § 7 (a). For equal protection clause, see, e.g.,
N.Y. Const. Art. 1, § 11.

4. Johnson v. Rankin, 70 N.C. 550, 555 (1874). See also Davis
v. R.R., 19 N.C. 451, 457-62 (1837).

5. DeBruhl v. State Highway and Public Works Comm'n, 247
N.C. 671, 675-76, 102 S.E.2d 229, 232-33 (1958).

6. See, e.g., Raleigh Mobile Homes Sales, Inc. v. Tomlinson,
267 NC 661, 174 S.E.2d 542 (1970).

7. State v. Dobbins, 277 N.C. 484, 178 S.E.2d 449 (1970).

8. Id. at 497, 178 S.E.2d at 456-57.

9. A recent major study of the taking issue concluded that the
popular conceptions as to the limitations imposed by the takings clause
were much more strict than those actually imposed by the courts. The
authors contend that this myth of the takings clause inhibits many local governments from adopting regulations which would in all likelihood
be upheld by the courts. F. Bosselman, D. Callies, and J. Banta, The
Taking Issue, infra note 11, at 323-24 (1973).

10. The Fifth Amendment prohibits the federal government from
committing the specified acts. The Fourteenth Amendment makes the
same prohibition applicable to the states: ". . . nor shall any state
deprive any person of life, liberty, or property, without due process
of law . . ." See Chicago, Burlington & Quincy Ry. v. Chicago, 166
U.S. 26 (1896).

11. Quoted in F. Bosselman, D. Callies, and J. Banta, The Taking
Issue: An Analysis of the Constitutional Limits of Land Use Control
62 (1973) [hereinafter cited as The Taking Issue].

12. Quoted in C. Harr, Land Use Planning: A Casebook on the
Use, Misuse, and Re-Use of Urban Land 413 (2d ed. 1971).

13. Boomer v. Atlantic Cement Co., 26 N.Y.2d 219, 257 N.E.2d
870, 309 N.Y.S.2d 312 (1970), damages awarded, permanent injunction
denied.

14. Pendoley v. Terreira, 345 Mass. 309, 187 N.E.2d 142 (1963),
injunction granted.

15. Schlotfelt v. Vinton Farmer's Supply Co., 252 Iowa 1102, 109
N.W.2d 695 (1961), injunction granted.

16. D. Hagman, Urban Planning and Land Development Control
Law § 158, at 289 (1971).

17. Village of Euclid v. Ambler Realty Co., 272 U.S. 365 (1926).

18. Michelman, "Property, Utility, and Fairness: Comments on the Ethical Foundations of 'Just Compensation' Law," 80 Harvard L. Rev. 1165 (1967).

19. 80 U.S. 166 (1871).

20. Id., at 177-78.

21. 99 U.S. 635(1898).

22. Id. at 642.

23. 123 U.S. 623 (1887).

24. Id. at 649.

25. Id. at 669.

26. 56 Wisc.2d 7, 201 N.W.2d 761 (1972).

27. Note, 86 Harvard L. Rev. 1582, 1585 (1973).

28. 56 Wisc.2d at 21.

29. See, e.g., Interstate Consol. St. Ry. v. Massachusetts, 207 U.S. 79 (1933); Hudson County Water Co. v. McCarter, 209 U.S. 349 (1935).

30. 260 U.S. 393 (1922).

31. Id. at 414-15.

32. Id. at 417.

33. 369 U.S. 590 (1962).

34. See, e.g., Hadacheck v. Sebastian, 239 U.S. 394 (1915); Erie Railroad v. Public Utilities Comm'rs., 254 U.S. 394 (1921).

35. Erie R.R. v. Public Utilities Comm'rs., supra note 34.

36. Sax, "Takings and the Police Power," 74 Yale L. J. 36, 42 (1964).

37. For more specific information on the following discussion, see Hagman, supra note 16, at §§ 137, 138, 140.

38. Hagman, supra note 16, at 253.

39. Id.

40. Id. at 254.

41. 18 N.Y.2d 78, 271 N.Y.S.2d 955 (1966).

42. 61 Misc.2d 619, 305 N.Y.S.2d 922 (N.Y. Sp. Ct. 1969).

43. See Just v. Marinette Co., 56 Wisc.2d 7 (1972).

44. See, e.g., Maine v. Johnson, 1 ERC 1353 (Me. 1970); Morris County Land Improvement Co. v. Parsippany-Troy Hills, 193 A.2d 232 (N.J. 1963); Dooley v. Town Planning and Zoning Commission, 197 A.2d 770 (Conn. 1964).

45. 11 Cal. App.3rd 557, 89 Ca. Rptr. 897 (1970).

46. 89 Cal. Rptr. at 905.

47. See, e.g., Rockland County Builders Ass'n., Inc. v. McAlvey, 37 App. Div. 2d 738, 324 N.Y.S.2d 190 (1970); rev'd., 30 N.Y.2d 359, 285 N.E.2d 291, 334 N.Y.S.2d 138 (1972).

48. 30 N.Y.2d 359, 285 N.E.2d 291, 334 N.Y.S.2d 138 (1972).

49. 57 Cal.2d 515, 370 P.2d 342, 20 Cal. Rptr. 638; appeal dismissed, 317 U.S. 36 (1962).

50. Note, 50 Calif. L. Rev. 896, 897 (1962).

51. Moroto Investment Co. Ltd. v. The County of Santa Cruz, No. 48607, Superior Court, Santa Cruz County, California, filed September 12, 1973.

52. Beyer v. City of Palo Alto, No. P22974, Superior Court, Santa Clara County, California, filed October 4, 1972.

53. 469 F.2d 956 (1st. Cir. 1972).

54. Id. at 961.

55. 419 Pa. 504, 215 A.2d 597 (1965), at 602-03.

56. Comment, "Equal Protection in Transition: An Analysis and a Proposal," 41 Fordham Law Review 605, 605-08 (1972).

57. Brown v. Board of Education of Topeka, 347 U.S. 483 (1954).

58. Baker v. Carr, 369 U.S. 186 (1962).

59. Glona v. American Guarantee & Liability Insurance Company, 391 U.S. 73 (1968).

60. Griffin v. Illinois, 351 U.S. 12 (1956).

61. Hawkins v. Town of Shaw, 461 F.2d 1171 (5th Cir. 1972) (en banc).

62. Crow v. Brown, 457 F.2d 788 (5th Cir. 1972).

63. Village of Belle Terre v. Boraas, 416 U.S. 1 (1974).

64. Norwalk Core v. Norwalk Redevelopment Agency, 395 F.2d 920 (2d Cir. 1968).

65. Pierro v. Baxendale, 20 N.J. 17, 26, 118 A.2d 401, 406 (1955).

66. Moose Lodge No. 107 v. Irvis, 407 U.S. 163 (1972).

67. 334 U.S. 1 (1948).

68. 387 U.S. 269, 375 (1967).

69. 436 F.2d 108, 112-14 (2d Cir. 1970) Cert. denied 401 U.S. 1010 (1970).

70. 493 F.2d 799 (5th Cir. 1974).

71. 200 Va. 653, 662, 107 S.E.2d 390, 396 (1959).

72. 107 R.I. 63, 264 A.2d 910 (1970).

73. Kennedy Park Homes v. City of Lackawanna, supra note 69, at 114.

74. Reynolds v. Sims, 377 U.S. 533, 561-62 (1964).

75. Shapiro v. Thompson, 394 U.S. 618, 634 (1969).

76. Skinner v. Oklahoma Ex rel. Williamson, 316 U.S. 535, 541 (1942).

77. "Congress shall make no law respecting an establishment of religion, prohibiting the free exercise thereof; or abridging the freedom of speech or of the press; or the right of the people peaceably to assemble, and to petition the government for a redress of grievance" (U.S. Const., Amend. 1).

78. Griffin v. Illinois, supra note 60.

79. Dandridge v. Williams, 397 U.S. 471 (1970).

80. Lindsey v. Normet, 405 U.S. 56, 74 (1972).

81. Harper v. Virginia State Board of Elections, 383 U.S. 663 (1966).

82. Shapiro v. Thompson, supra note 75, at 634.

83. Mclaughlin v. Florida, 379 U.S. 184 (1964).

84. Hernandez v. Texas, 347 U.S. 475 (1954).

85. Gautreauz v. Chicago Housing Authority, 296 F. Supp. 907, 914 (N.D. ILL. 1969). For more recent developments in this case see Gautreaux v. Chicago Housing Authority, 503 F.2d 930 (1974).

86. Allied Stores of Ohio v. Bowers, 358 U.S. 522 (1958).

87. Cole v. Housing Authority of City of Newport, 435 F.2d 807 (1st. Cir. 1970).

88. See, e.g., Hawkins v. Town of Shaw, 461 F.2d 1171 (5th. Cir. 1972) (en banc).

89. Dunn v. Blumstein, 405 U.S. 330, 343 (1972).

90. See, e.g., National Land and Investment Co. v. Kohn, 419 Pa. 504, 215 A.2d 597 (1967).

91. Dunn v. Blumstein, 405 U.S. 330 (1972).

92. Eggert v. City of Seattle, 505 P.2d 801 (1973).

93. Cole v. Housing Authority, 435 F.2d 807 (1st. Cir. 1970).

94. Strans v. Malkerson, 326 F. Supp. 234 (D. Minn 1970) Aff'd, 401 U.S. 985 (1971).

95. Memorial Hospital v. Maricopa County, 415 U.S. 250 (1974).

96. Construction Industry Association of Sonoma County v. City of Petaluma, 375 F. Supp. 574 (N.D. Cal. 1974). The ultimate impact of the right to travel on managed growth will not be known until the United States Supreme Court rules on the issue. However, in at least one case, Village of Belle Terre v. Boraas, 416 U.S. 1, 7 (1974), the Supreme Court is on record as saying that the right to travel applies to transients and is not aimed at zoning ordinances.

97. Construction Industry Association of Sonoma Co. v. City of Petaluma, F.2d (9th. Cir. 1975). A petition for review by the Supreme Court has been filed. The finding of a lack of standing was largely based on Warth v. Seldin, _____ U.S. _____ (1975).

98. 6 F. Cas. 546, 552 (No. 3230) (C.C.E.D. Pa. 1823).

99. 73 U.S. 35, 43-44 (1868).

100. Williams v. Fear, 179 U.S. 270 (1900).

101. Kent v. Dulles, 357 U.S. 116 (1958).

102. Edwards v. California, 314 U.S. 160 (1941).

103. 378 U.S. 500 (1964).

104. Dombrowski v. Pfister, 380 U.S. 479, 486-89 (1964).

105. Shapiro v. Thompson, supra note 75, at 618, 642-44 (1969) (concurring opinion).

106.  United States v. Guest, 383 U.S. 745 (1966).

107.  394 U.S. 618 (1969).

108.  326 F. Supp. 234 (D. Minn 1970) Aff'd, 401 U.S. 985 (1971).

109.  93 Cal Rptr 786 (Dist. Ct. App. 1971).

110.  435 F.2d 807 (1st. Cir. 1970).

111.  King v. New Rochelle, 442 F.2d 646, 648 (2d Cir. 1971) Cert. denied, 404 U.S. 863 (1971).

112.  394 U.S. at 638.

113.  Id. at 627.

114.  Id. at 633.

115.  Id.

116.  Id. at 633-34.

117.  Zeml v. Rusk, 381 U.S. 1, 15-16 (1965).

118.  United States v. Chalk, 441 F.2d 1277, 1283 (4th Cir. 1971). Cert. denied, 409 U.S. 943 (1972).

119.  338 F. Supp. 492, 499-501 (1972).

# 3

## SELECTED TOOLS
## AND TECHNIQUES OF
## DEVELOPMENT TIMING

LARGE LOT ZONING

The Large Lot Zoning Concept

As communities begin to struggle with the problems attendant upon an increasingly rapid rate of growth, their first response is often to increase lot size requirements in their zoning ordinances.

A community's power to impose such a limitation is sustained by the basic and well-established exercise of the police power granted to localities by the state.[1] Most state zoning enabling acts allow localities to regulate the size of yards and density of population in order to reduce congestion in streets, promote health and the general welfare, prevent overcrowding of land, avoid undue concentration of population, and facilitate the adequate provision of transportation, water, sewage, schools, parks, and other public requirements.[2] Thus, states usually have specifically granted localities the power to regulate lot sizes via their zoning ordinances.

Many communities react to rapid growth by restricting development to single-family homes on lots ranging from one to six or more acres. This restriction, which is often used in conjunction with other density-limiting devices such as minimum floor-area requirements, is most often imposed in outlying fringe areas that are either undeveloped or just beginning to show serious developmental pressures.

Until the early 1940s, most urban residential development took either the form of apartments, or houses on small lots. Lots occupying an acre or more were rare.[3] However, in the period following World War II, the use of large lot zoning has become common. Following a 1942 Massachusetts case, Simon v. Needham, which upheld a

zoning ordinance with requirements for one-acre minimum lot sizes,
many communities began to require larger lots for development.[4] In
1962 it was estimated that nearly one-half of all the vacant land zoned
for residential use in the New York metropolitan region was zoned for
lots of one acre or larger.[5] Given the high degree of municipal fragmentation in many urban areas, a number of suburbs began to adopt
large lot zoning as a defensive measure, fearing that if they fell behind in the zoning race, they might "quickly become a target for mass
developers catering to the less wealthy spectrum of the homebuying
market, thus burdening it with unusually fast development and a loss
of relative prestige."[6] A current example of the overuse of large lot
zoning is found in St. Louis County, Missouri. There it is estimated
that given the present level of demand, there is a 350-year supply of
lots of one acre or larger, but only a four-year supply of lots of one-
third acre or smaller.[7]

It is important at the outset to distinguish two differing applications of the large lot zoning concept. First, it may be used as a temporary barrier to intensive residential development, establishing
what in effect are holding zones. The second use of the tool involves
the community actively planning to have only low density residential
development as the ultimate use of the land so zoned. It is often very
difficult to ascertain whether a particular ordinance is intended to
enact temporary or permanent large lot zoning, because few make
such a distinction on their face. However, the distinction is crucial
because each type of zoning implies objectives that are entirely distinct from those of the other.

The use of large lot zoning as a temporary bar to residential
construction is a direct attempt by the community to control the timing of urban development. With this approach, intensive residential
development is not entirely prohibited; rather, it is postponed until
the community can accommodate it.[8] That zoning has potential for use
as a timing device has been recognized for some time. A 1961 report
concluded that communities could "utilize upgraded zoning to discourage development in the outlying districts while permitting more
intensive use of land closer to the urban center. At the same time,
the peripheral districts are designated for change to lower minimums
once the initial lands near full utilization."[9] The idea was to use
large lot zoning as a means of encouraging urban infilling. Recently,
a consultant's report to the Maryland National Capital Parks and
Planning Commission recommended that large parts of the Washington, D.C. metropolitan area be zoned for ten-acre minimum lot sizes
in order to create holding zones, thus allowing direct governmental
control over the timing of development.[10] Closely related to these
proposals is the practice, adopted by a number of communities of

establishing holding zones, by zoning large areas for nonresidential uses such as agriculture.

The holding zone concept has several primary uses. First, it can be used to prevent development from taking place in those areas which are as yet inadequately served by public facilities such as water and sewer lines, roads, schools, and recreational facilities.[11] Second, the holding zone is also effective as an interim control device, pending the adoption of permanent zoning controls.[12] In this situation, the community wishes to prevent any intensive development while planning efforts are underway and permanent regulatory schemes are being devised; it uses large lot zoning as, in effect, an undeclared moratorium on community growth. Finally, communities may establish holding zones to insure that all development proposals will come under their review. All developers must petition for rezoning, a requirement that sets up a system for the city to prohibit or allow growth on a case-by-case basis.

In addition to its temporary use, large lot zoning can be used to establish the permanent character of undeveloped land. In this way, it can be used to prohibit development which would otherwise encroach upon prime agricultural land or other valuable open space. It can similarly be used to protect environmentally sensitive areas.[13]

In addition to these protection objectives, residents of non-urban areas may wish to preserve the character of their community—its visual beauty and its quiet, uncongested way of living, with ample room for children, leisure activities, and privacy.[14] Further, such zoning may be imposed for fiscal reasons. Many localities believe expansive houses on large lots will provide a return on public investment in providing services, while high-density housing represents a loss.[15] Finally, since explicit racial[16] and social[17] exclusion is illegal, some communities seek to price out "undesirables" with large lot zoning. Undoubtedly, the courts will find large lot zoning based on such motivations "sterile and undemocratic,"[18] and will overturn such regulatory schemes.

## Impacts of Large Lot Zoning

Large lot zoning affects both the rate of development and its patterns of location. It also can significantly influence the economic and social character of both the community using it and the areas surrounding that community. However, pinpointing which effects or what part of them are directly attributable to large lot zoning is not possible. Also, the actual impact will vary with each application of

the tool, depending upon the pressures for growth in the individual
community, the minimum size of lots used, the relative amount of
land so zoned, the length of time the land is left in such zones, and
a number of other localized factors. Thus, the following general observations can only be starting points for analysis.

## Temporal Effects

By placing much of a community's vacant land in large lot zones,
premature intensive residential development can be forestalled. However, this action allows no flexibility for meeting future changes in the
community's needs. In addition, summarily zoning all vacant land in
the same way forecloses a responsiveness to differing pressures, and
to the varying capacities of individual parcels of land. For this reason, when a high percentage of vacant land is put into large lot zones,
the political pressure for individual rezonings can be overwhelming.
Of course, the requirement that all landowners who wish to develop
must request a rezoning gives the community greater leverage in requiring that proposed developments be of an "acceptable" quality, but
such a discretionary review mechanism also carries the potential for
political abuse.

Finally, it should be noted that the rate of growth is not necessarily slowed by increasing lot sizes.[19] Increasing lot sizes may in
fact sometimes have the opposite effect, making the area more attractive to potential homebuyers and thereby inducing development.

In a survey of planning agencies active in efforts to time development (described in detail in Chapter 4), large lot zoning was rated
a relatively ineffective device for development timing. Of the 39 respondents who presently use or have used large lot zoning (defined as
lot minimums of two or more acres), only 23 percent rated it "very
effective." Thirty-eight percent said it was "moderately effective,"
23 percent said "slightly effective," and a full 15 percent said it was
"not effective" in controlling the timing of development in their jurisdictions.

## Spatial Effects

Large lot zoning, if unaltered, requires residential development
to be of very low density—single-family homes on large lots. But unless the lot sizes are ten acres or more, the appearance is one of
urban sprawl, not of a rural or small town setting.

A rural appearance will not necessarily result from large lot
zoning.[20] Development of single-family homes on one-acre lots often
produces uniform, unpleasing tract subdivisions rather than the contemplated result of homes nestled in idyllic settings. Large lot zoning
can also consume land at an extremely rapid rate.

These factors have led some observers to conclude that large lot zoning produces aesthetic atrocities and wastes land inexcusably.[21] Such a result is entirely possible if large lot zoning is imposed on a permanent basis.

## Economic Effects

If large lot zoning is adopted only as a temporary bar to development, there can be fiscal savings for the community without serious adverse economic impacts for the residents. Such a strategy, by limiting premature residential development, allows the community to phase the provision of urban services in the most rational, cost-effective manner. Since higher residential densities will be allowed only as services are provided, the adverse economic impacts on individual residents are minimized. In fact, the residents may well benefit, because the increased fiscal stability of local governments and the rational provision of urban services may lead to lower tax rates.

However, if large lot zoning is applied on a permanent basis, the economic impacts on both local government and community residents are more problematical. In fact, a recent study of the St. Louis County, Missouri area estimates that additional expenditures by local governments and homeowners on the order of $1 million per year are attributable to large lot zoning.[22]

Long-term fiscal savings for local governments that enact large lot zoning ordinances are uncertain at best.[23] The per capita cost of providing services may even be higher. With large lot development, some urban services, such as mass transit and water and sewer systems, become inefficient and quite costly, if indeed they are feasible at all.[24]

The effect on the individual property owner can be more direct and more dramatic. While large lot zoning may serve to protect property values for present residents, it will in all likelihood drive up housing costs for future residents. First, raw land costs will rise for two reasons—the lot itself is larger, and more importantly, the absolute number of lots available for development is fixed.[25] Generally, "competition among developers for the potential sites will be more intense, as their number is more limited. More competition for fewer sites will inflate prices, increase densities, or both."[26] Here, as low density levels are maintained by the minimum lot size requirements, prices will rise. Secondly, housing costs will rise for future residents because site improvement costs rise with the size of the lot. In many cases developers tie the size and cost of a house being built to the size of the lot. A third element of the rise in housing costs is the increased cost of maintenance. And finally, if the house and lot are indeed more expensive than would otherwise be the case, the homeowner will face increased property taxes. Related to this are increased transportation costs which the homeowner must expect to pay given the "spread" character of development. There will, in all likelihood be less mass transit, longer work-residence trips, and increased need for a second car. Because of the increased price of energy, this rise in transportation costs may be quite substantial.

Finally, the social implications of the rise in housing costs should be noted. If housing costs are substantially raised, the already serious problems of social and racial residential segregation in our society will be exacerbated. This adverse social impact must be closely monitored and controlled if communities are going to manage their growth in an equitable manner.

### Legal Limitations on the Use of Large Lot Zoning

The statutory authority for localities to regulate lot size through zoning is clearly granted in most state zoning enabling acts.[27] Given the presumption of validity that such acts are granted by the courts,[28] and the explicit nature of the grant of power, it seems highly unlikely that large lot zoning schemes will be overturned on statutory grounds.[29] However, they are an exercise of the police power, and as such are subject to fundamental constitutional limitations on the kind and extent of regulations which the government may impose.[30] The individual is protected from governmental overreach by the constitutional guarantees of the due process and equal protection of the laws as well as by the constitutionally implied right to travel and migration.[31]

The basic due process requirement is that all governmental exercises of the police power must be rationally related to permissible governmental objectives. More simply, the regulation must serve a legitimate purpose or it will be declared invalid.

If a large lot zoning scheme is found to be directed toward social and racial exclusion, or is simply intended to hold local taxes down, it will be overturned because these are clearly not permissible governmental objectives. However, a desire to time development so as to assure the availability of adequate public services is a permissible objective. This is so largely because of its relationship to a basic permissible objective—protecting community health.

Large lot zoning is often justified as an attempt to protect the public health and safety, as communities know that these are legitimate governmental objectives.[32] However, the lot sizes generally necessary to establish meaningful holding zones clearly exceed those which can be regarded as essential for health and safety.[33] If one-acre lots are suitable for septic tanks, the town will be hard pressed to justify five-acre lot zoning. This is particularly true in fringe developing areas. A noted legal scholar has concluded that, while large lot zoning may be upheld in rural areas, the situation is different in developing areas:

> Courts react adversely in developing areas and recognize the devices as intended to prevent people in the low income bracket from moving in, that large minimums tend to promote sprawl and that while septic tanks, wells, and roads may not be adequate, local government is obligated to provide sewer, water and road systems. The needs of people for living space are more important than status quoism, preserving rural character or providing greenbelts.[34]

The regulation, to be upheld, must also be rationally related to a permissible objective similar to those mentioned above. To establish a relationship between objective and regulation does not pose a difficult problem for local governments. Courts have generally ruled that any rational relationship to a permissible objective is adequate. For the most part, the courts defer to legislative judgment in these cases,[35] but, as it is largely a matter of case-by-case review, it is impossible to generalize about the outcome of a judicial challenge to a specific ordinance.

A second major potential limitation on due process grounds on large lot zoning is the recent expanded reading of the general welfare clause of the Constitution by some state courts, particularly the Pennsylvania and New Jersey Supreme Courts.[36] The reasoning is that since the localities are exercising a state power when they zone, they must act to further the general welfare of the state as a whole, rather than only that of a particular locality.[37] If the local ordinance does not relate to regional considerations, the court may find that the community is attempting to effectuate an impermissible objective, and is thus violating due process.

The final potential due process challenge is one based on the prohibition against the taking of private property by the government without the payment of due compensation. As large lot zoning generally allows the landowner to make productive use of the property so zoned, it seems unlikely that a "taking" challenge would be successful. If the locality were to use extremely large lot zones, however—for example, in the order of fifty to sixty-acre lots—a "taking" challenge would not be unrealistic.

The two other constitutional provisions which may be relevant here are the equal protection clause and the right to travel. If a

particular ordinance made unreasonable or arbitrary distinctions between two similarly situated landowners it could be overturned on
equal protection grounds. Moreover, if such a distinction infringes
upon a fundamental constitutional right, the courts will strictly scruti-
nize the ordinance in question to determine whether a "compelling
state interest" justified the distinction. The right to travel is such a
fundamental interest.[38] If it can be established that large lot zoning
infringes upon the constitutionally protected right to travel, the burden
is placed upon the locality to produce a compelling justification for
the infringement. The court will ask whether a more tightly drawn
ordinance could achieve the same objectives with less infringement
upon constitutional rights.

Since large lot zoning has been so widely adopted, several commentators have recommended that state governments find legislative
and administrative solutions to the wide range of legal and constitutional problems involved with it, so that communities will not have to
rely on the judiciary to tell them when they have overstepped their
constitutional bounds.[39] One legislative resolution of many of these
problems would be to set a statutory ceiling on lot size zoning. This,
however, does not provide the flexibility needed in local planning control. And the minimum size chosen would probably become the standard lot size throughout the state, and because of that would provide
little protection for those excluded by large lot zoning.

A more attractive solution would be to establish a state-wide
review board to replace trial-level courts in hearing challenges to
proposed large lot zoning schemes. The legislature could then establish a benchmark lot size (for example, one-half an acre or one acre)
and require localities to receive special permission from the board
before setting any lot size requirements above this figure. Individuals
aggrieved by a particular ordinance would be able to challenge even
lot size requirements of the benchmark size or lower if they felt that
they were unjustified.[40] This approach avoids the rigidity of a statutory ceiling, allows a speedy administrative adjudication of any conflict, and insures that regional interests will be protected in the course
of local zoning control.


## THE ADEQUATE PUBLIC FACILITIES ORDINANCE


Public efforts to control the rate of urban development have for
the most part been unsuccessful. The critical decisions in the development process have generally been made by private businessmen and
developers who are "rarely committed to the best interests of the entire community."[41]

The results of this lack of control over development are painfully evident today. Rampant growth has outstripped the capacity of many communities to provide necessary urban services. Schools, roads, parks, and recreational facilities have become overcrowded. Serious environmental damage has resulted from a lack of sanitary sewer facilities. Following periods of unmanaged growth, increases in real property tax rates have been needed to keep pace with efforts to provide these necessary facilities. Other closely related problems include the unpleasant aesthetic results of poor design and haphazard development, and a large degree of wasteful speculation in the private land market.[42]

## The Adequate Public Facilities Concept

For the above reasons, several communities have sought to place a moratorium on development until adequate public services are available, thus stabilizing capital expenditures and taxing structures.[43] One method of accomplishing this is the adequate public facilities ordinance, which explicitly controls the rate of urban development by limiting the issuance of building permits to those areas adequately served by public facilities. By tying the ordinance to a long-range capital improvements plan, each property owner can know when he will be able to develop his land. Thus the ordinance does not seek to avoid or deny problems of population expansion. It is not necessarily anti-growth. Rather it seeks to channel growth into those areas in which it can best be accommodated. The ordinance, if properly designed and administered, is used to stage growth, not to stop it.[44]

The concept of public control over the timing of development is not a new one.[45] In a 1955 article, Henry Fagin pointed out five justifications for the imposition of timing controls: (1) the need to economize on the costs of municipal facilities and services; (2) the need to retain municipal control over the eventual character of development; (3) the need to maintain a desirable balance among various uses of land; (4) the need to achieve greater detail and specificity in development regulation; and (5) the need to maintain a high quality in community services and facilities.[46] Fagin concluded his article with the contention that

. . . the mass of mounting evidence eloquently argues that regulating the timing of urban development is a valid and necessary exercise of the police power. Such regulation

not only is permissible in the legal sense but has become
an urgent responsibility of municipal government needed
to protect the very health, safety, and welfare of our rapidly growing suburban communities.[47]

## The Ramapo Application

Direct public regulation of the timing of development remained
a theoretical construct before the late 1960s, when the Township of
Ramapo, New York, adopted it as a policy.

The Township of Ramapo is a suburban and rural area consisting of about 50 square miles of unincorporated land located in Rockland County, approximately 25 miles north of midtown Manhattan.
There are several incorporated villages within the township, and under
New York law they exercise exclusive control over land use within
their respective jurisdictions. During the 1960s, the township came
under severe development pressure, largely because of the increased
accessibility to New York City resulting from the construction of the
New York State Thruway, the Tappan Zee Bridge, and the extension
of the Garden State Parkway to the Thruway.[48] The population of
Ramapo more than doubled between 1960 and 1970.[49]

Following the election of a new township administration in 1965,
concerted efforts were initiated to control this tremendous rate of
growth. Extensive studies of land use, public facilities, transportation, industry, commerce, housing, and population trends were undertaken.[50] This led to the adoption of a master development plan in
1966, which proposed holding the township's population increase at a
moderate rate in order to preserve its "rural, semi-rural and suburban character."[51]

During the six-month period between the adoption of this development plan and the enactment of a comprehensive zoning ordinance,
the town board approved an Interim Development Ordinance that placed
a moratorium on the issuance of all building permits in certain areas
of the township.[52] The Comprehensive Zoning Ordinance which followed was of the traditional Euclidean type. It designated over 90 percent of the township's area for residential use, much of it in zones
with large minimum lot sizes. There was no provision in the ordinance for multi-family housing, with the exception of housing for the
elderly, in buffer zones between areas reserved for single-family
and commercial uses.[53]

The township's next step, following the completion of additional
sewage and drainage studies, was the adoption of a six-year Capital
Budget which provided for the development of the improvements called

for in the Master Plan. As a supplement to this Capital Budget, the
township also adopted a Capital Program which specified the location
and sequence of further capital improvements in the 12 years following
the life of the Capital Budget. These two plans cover a period of 18
years, at the end of which the township expected to have reached its
maximum development capacity, with all needed public services having been provided.[54]

In order to assure that the pace of private development would
not exceed that contemplated in the above-mentioned plans, the township in 1969 adopted an Amended Zoning Ordinance.[55] This is the
adequate public facilities ordinance that has since attracted nationwide attention. The ordinance prohibits any residential development,
unless the developer first obtains a special use permit from the town
board.[56] Such a permit is to be issued only if the proposed development earns 15 "development points," computed and awarded on sliding scales (scored from zero to five), based on the proximity of the
development to the following public facilities and services: (1) public
sewers or approved substitutes, (2) drainage capacity, (3) improved
public park or recreational facilities, including public school sites,
(4) state, county, or town roads improved with curbs and sidewalks,
and (5) fire houses.[57] The township thus tied the right to develop residential areas to the presence of these municipal improvements.

By examining the capital budget and program, a developer can
readily ascertain when his particular parcel will accumulate a sufficient number of points to receive a permit for residential development. In order to establish a high degree of certainty, the ordinance
provides that the town board shall, upon application, issue a special
permit vesting a present right for the developer to proceed with his
proposed development at such time as the current plan indicates
enough points will become available.[58] Thus the right to develop is
tied to the scheduled completion date of the proposed capital improvements, rather than to the date of their actual provision. Furthermore,
the developer can advance this date by agreeing to provide at his own
expense such improvements as will earn the development the required
number of points.[59]

The effect of this ordinance is to prohibit residential development until the requisite supporting facilities are available. According to the capital improvement program, this can mean that development may be deferred for as long as 18 years in some areas of the
township. The township contends that it is not eliminating future
growth in its jurisdiction, but is only deferring development rights
on a temporary basis—that is, until necessary services are available.
The ordinance further provides for a reassessment of tax valuations
that would take into account any reduction in property values resulting

from these temporal restrictions on the development of the land. It is
for these reasons that the town claims the ordinance merely stages
urban development, and is not confiscatory.

Ramapo's plan for development timing was promptly challenged
in court by a coalition of landowners and homebuilders.[60] They contended that the town had exceeded the zoning powers and objectives
granted to it by the state; that the ordinance constituted an uncompen-
sated taking of private property; and that its exclusion of new residents
from the community constituted a violation of equal protection of the
law. On May 3, 1972, New York's highest court, in Golden v. Planning
Bd. of the Township of Ramapo, reversed a lower court and upheld the
validity of the Ramapo ordinance in a five-to-two decision.[61] Robert
Freilich, who had drafted the ordinance, hailed this judicial upholding
of a restriction on development through planning, without compensation, as "perhaps the most important advance in zoning law since the
watershed case of Euclid v. Ambler."[62] Other reactions, both to the
development timing ordinance in itself and to its particular application
in Ramapo, have been less enthusiastic.[63] But virtually all observers
agree that the Ramapo decision is one of great significance, and that
the adequate public facilities ordinance, with its multifaceted implications for the future of American planning regulation, is worthy of
increased attention and evaluation.


Limitations on the Use of the Adequate Public Facilities Ordinance


Before examining the impacts of the adequate public facilities
ordinance, it will be helpful to examine some of the factors which may
well limit its use as a growth management tool. There is considerable
debate among legal authorities as to whether local governmental units
have the statutory authority to impose a development timing ordinance
at all, and, if they do, whether its use would violate provisions of the
United States Constitution. In addition to these legal problems, the
high level of technical expertise required to design the ordinance, and
the political realities of local developmental regulation may create
serious impediments to the widespread use of the techniques.

Statutory Limitations

The power to zone and otherwise regulate development resides
with the state. Local governments have no inherent powers to zone
their territory. They possess only such power to zone as is delegated
to them by state enabling legislation.[64] If the local zoning scheme

exceeds the scope of authority granted by the state, the local ordinance will be found to be ultra vires and thus invalid.

The development timing ordinance is subject to an ultra vires challenge on several grounds. First, it can be contended that the state has not specifically granted localities the power to directly regulate the timing of development. Secondly, there is the issue of whether the purpose for which an ordinance is adopted is one which is authorized by the legislation. Finally, there is a statutory requirement that all zoning regulations shall be made in accordance with a comprehensive plan.[65] The first two of these issues are closely related, and comprised the central issue in the litigation on Ramapo's development timing plan.

The New York enabling legislation construed in Golden is very closely modeled after the Standard State Zoning Enabling Act promulgated by the Department of Commerce in the early 1920s.[66] The delegation of power to the localities is contained in the first section of the Standard Act, and the permissible purposes of zoning regulations are enumerated in Section Three. The relevant portions are as follows:

> Section 1. Grant of Power — For the purpose of promoting health, safety, morals, or general welfare of the community, the legislative body of cities and incorporated villages is hereby empowered to regulate and restrict the height, number of stories, and size of buildings and other structures, the percentage of lot that may be occupied, the size of yards, courts, and other open spaces, the density of population, and the location and use of buildings, structures, and land for trade, industry, residence, or other purposes.[67]

> Section 3. Purposes in View — Such regulation shall be made in accordance with a comprehensive plan and be designed to lessen congestion in the streets; to secure safety from fire, panic, and other dangers; to promote health and general welfare; to provide adequate light and air; to prevent the overcrowding of land; to avoid undue concentration of population; to facilitate the adequate provision of transportation, water, sewerage, schools, parks, and other public requirements.[68] (Emphasis added.)

The first question for consideration then is whether, under such a state enabling act, a locality has the power to enact an adequate public facilities ordinance. The fact that this is a very close and difficult question is aptly illustrated by the course of holdings in the

Ramapo litigation. There, the trial judge held that the power granted "obviously . . . includes the power to regulate growth of population."[69] In the appellate division, the sharply divided court's reversal turned squarely on the ultra vires challenge; the court found that "the power to place time controls on a municipality's population expansion, as in the instant case, has not yet been delegated."[70] Finally, the New York Court of Appeals (the state's highest court) reversed the lower appeals court and sustained the use of time controls on development. While recognizing the lack of express statutory authorization for an ordinance of this type, the court inferred such a power, holding that "The power to restrict and regulate conferred under [Section 1] includes within its grant, by way of necessary implication, the authority to direct the growth of population for the purposes indicated."[71] This implies that if the court finds the purposes of the ordinance valid (as determined by compliance with Section 3), it will hold that the power to achieve those purposes must, by implication, exist.

The dissent filed with the Golden decision sharply disagreed with this conclusion. It contended that the grant of powers section of the enabling act clearly did not grant Ramapo the power to impose a moratorium on land development through its adequate public facilities ordinance.[72] The dissent also held that the purposes section of the enabling act was designed to restrict the powers section by requiring all local regulations to be directly related to the specified purposes, not broaden it as was contended by the majority.[73]

The question of whether the adequate public facilities ordinance serves a valid or permissible purpose is easier to resolve. As was emphasized in the quotation above, the Standard Act allows regulation designed to "facilitate the adequate provision of transportation, water, sewerage, schools, parks, and other public requirements." As the Ramapo ordinance was, on its face, strictly an attempt to assure that development only takes place where there are adequate public facilities of the enumerated type, it seems clearly to come within the ambit of this specified purpose.

This enunciated purpose should, however, be distinguished from an objective of entirely stopping the population growth of an area. This may be an effect of a particular adequate public facilities ordinance, but it is not a valid justification for its imposition.

The final statutory requirement for a local adequate public facilities ordinance is that it be made "in accordance with a comprehensive plan."[74] This requirement is imposed to assure that zoning regulations will be used as a means to a previously defined end, rather than as ends in themselves. The requirement is rather straightforward, and generally poses no problem for local development regulation. However, it should be noted that there is a growing trend by state courts to require land use regulations to be consistent with previously adopted plans.[75]

It is of course impossible to foretell how other state courts would deal with the ultra vires questions which would arise with the adoption of adequate public facilities ordinances. Whether they would be willing to adopt the liberal reading of the enabling legislation, as the New York Court did in the Golden decision, is an open question which can only be answered by future litigation. As is the case with any new planning technique, localities will have to proceed cautiously in their use of the adequate public facilities ordinance, pending judicial ratification of its validity.

## Constitutional Limitations

Once it is determined that the statutory authority to enact adequate public facilities ordinances exists, legal challenges may turn on the constitutional issues involved. There are four potential major constitutional limitations on the use of these ordinances: substantive due process; the taking issue;[76] equal protection requirements;[77] and potential infringement on the right to travel.[78]

(1) Due process requirements for the police power. The due process provisions of the United States Constitution[79] require invalidation of any local ordinance, even if enacted within the scope of the state enabling legislation, that is not reasonably related to permissible state objectives. As a general rule, courts now will usually adopt a posture of judicial restraint when considering this point, preferring to defer to legislative judgment that the relationship between the regulation and the objectives to be served is sufficient.[80] Thus, an exercise of the police power is generally said to be cloaked with a presumption of validity. Still, if a court is unable to find any rational relationship between the regulation and a permissible governmental objective, the ordinance will be struck down. It seems that the adequate public facilities ordinance is in no way seriously threatened by this nexus requirement, as it can be quite directly related to the community's zoning objectives of systematic, orderly development.[81]

Other attempts by local government to deal with population growth, particularly requirements for large minimum lot sizes, have been successfully attacked on the grounds that they had such exclusionary impacts, not justifiable as efforts to further the health, safety, morals, or general welfare of the community, that they violated the due process clause.[82] If the court found that an ordinance was aimed at halting population growth, freezing development, excluding racial minorities or particular economic groups, or simply was an attempt to avoid the fiscal burdens attendant upon an increased demand for municipal facilities, the ordinance might well be voided as an attempt to effectuate impermissible objectives.

Finally, some state courts, particularly those of New Jersey and Pennsylvania,[83] have adopted a reading of the state enabling acts which requires localities to give greater attention to regional housing needs.[84] The constitutional argument there adopted is as follows. Localities have no inherent power to zone or otherwise regulate development.[85] They may act only in accordance with the state enabling act, which delegates to the localities the power to regulate development in order to promote their "health, safety, and general welfare." As the power which is being delegated is one which is inherently held by the state, the "general welfare" referred to is that of the state as a whole. If the general welfare being promoted by a particular regulatory scheme is only that of the locality imposing it, then the permissible governmental objective of promoting the general welfare of the state is not being served. Rather, the locality is merely promoting its own welfare, possibly to the detriment of the welfare of the state. So the regulation is said to be designed to effectuate an impermissible governmental objective, and is thus void, as a violation of the due process of law. A local adequate public facilities ordinance developed without a regional perspective might be held unconstitutional on these grounds.

(2) The taking issue. The United States Constitution prohibits government from taking private property for public use without just compensation. If an otherwise valid regulation so restricts the private use of land that the courts deem it to be a confiscation, compensation must be paid to the private land owner or the ordinance will fall. The question of exactly at what point regulation turns into taking is a subject of intense legal debate and cannot be resolved by resort to mathematical formulas.[86]

There is no doubt that an adequate public facilities ordinance restricts the private use of land. The plaintiffs in the Golden case contended that this restriction amounted to a taking, because residential development was prohibited in some areas for as long as 18 years. Since they, as property owners, were not compensated for this restriction, they asked the court to invalidate Ramapo's ordinance as an unconstitutional taking of private property.[87]

The New York court disagreed with this contention. It held that while Ramapo's restrictions on residential development were substantial, they were not absolute. The ordinance did not permanently prevent development, it only deferred it for a certain definite period, which in some cases was as long as 18 years. Since all property could eventually be developed, the court held these restrictions to be temporary, and therefore not a taking for which compensation would be required.

(3) Equal protection of the law. The United States Constitution prohibits a state from denying the equal protection of the law to any person within its jurisdiction. This does not mean that all inequalities and classifications are prohibited. The prohibition extends only to those classifications deemed to be arbitrary and unreasonable.[88]

The adequate public facilities concept creates classifications by its very nature. Some property owners may develop their land immediately, while others are forced to postpone development for varying lengths of time. It therefore must be asked whether this distinction is unconstitutionally discriminatory, in the sense of being arbitrary and unreasonable. A properly designed ordinance prohibits development only where there are insufficient urban services available. Thus the distinction is a nonarbitrary, reasonable one, which is closely related to a legitimate zoning end, and is not a violation of equal protection.

This is not to imply that all adequate public facilities ordinances will be free from equal protection challenges. If the ordinance is applied in a manner which creates a distinction between similarly situated developers, a valid equal protection argument arises. Also, if the effect of the ordinance is to limit the housing opportunities of racial minorities, then the locality may have to demonstrate a compelling state interest to justify the distinction.[89] In essence, not only must the concept meet the equal protection requirements, but the individual applications of each ordinance must also be accomplished in a manner which is not arbitrary or unreasonable.

(4) The right to travel. Recent United States Supreme Court decisions have made it clear that individuals have a constitutionally protected right to interstate travel and migration which cannot be unduly restricted by state or local controls on the use of land.[90] The adequate public facilities ordinance does not directly prohibit all inmigration, as is the case with the various development moratoria. But it does limit the timing and the overall amount of development which can take place. By providing for only a low level of urban services, a locality can make this limitation a severe one. To what extent the courts will examine the density patterns underlying the ordinance or require localities to provide additional levels of urban service in order to prevent undue restrictions on the right to travel, is an open question which can only be answered by appropriate litigation.

## Limitations of Technical Capabilities

The adequate public facilities ordinance, while relatively simple, is in practice an exacting tool which requires a substantial amount of preparatory and supportive work. The high degree of planning,

administrative, and legal skills required for its meaningful application
could deter many communities' use of the device. Also, it is particularly unsuited to the practice of widespread adoption of a single general model. It must be carefully fitted to the needs and capabilities of
each locality considering its use.

The first step required for use of the ordinance is the preparation of complete studies of existing land uses, public facilities, transportation networks, and housing availabilities. Accurate future growth
projections are also needed to determine demand levels for all types
of land use. Finally, a comprehensive plan or set of future decision
guides should be prepared.

A realistic and workable long-term capital improvements schedule is the first prerequisite for actual implementation of an adequate
public facilities ordinance. As the twin aims of the tool are to first
prohibit development where adequate public facilities are not available
and secondly to provide landowners with a definite idea of when their
land can be developed, the capital improvement program must be detailed and it must be approved before the tool can be used. This schedule should reflect the comprehensive plan, and it should be coordinated
with the proposed spatial allocation of land uses within the area. Most
careful attention should be given to this schedule because, when tied
to an adequate public facilities ordinance, it directly sets the rate of
development in the jurisdiction adopting it.

Also, it is likely that communities adopting an adequate public
facilities approach will require significant levels of legal assistance
in the development and, possibly, the defense of their ordinances
against judicial challenges. As was discussed at length above, there
are rather strict statutory and constitutional issues which must be
satisfactorily resolved before a development timing plan can be
adopted. As each local effort to use the tool must be fitted within
those constraints, legal counsel and advice is necessary at an early
point in the planning process and should continue throughout.

## Political Limitations

The final limitation on the use of the adequate public facilities
ordinance is a very practical one—its political acceptability. Developers will generally stand ready to oppose any limitations on their
ability to build what they want at the time they want to build it. Landowners, particularly those who will be prevented from developing
their land for a considerable period of time, may well resent this
new exercise of governmental control. Local government leaders
themselves may react adversely to the ordinance's lack of flexibility
once implemented, and to the necessarily implied explicit statements
as to just what development will be allowed, and when it will be allowed
to take place.

Still, if there is widespread understanding on the part of the community and its leaders as to what the ordinance actually does and how it may properly be used, then the desire to manage rationally the community's growth can outweigh these political impediments.

## Impacts

The impacts of an adequate public facilities ordinance, both intended and actual, are widespread. The ordinance has important direct effects on both the rate of development and the spatial character of development in the jurisdiction adopting it. Its use also has significant environmental, economic, and social implications. Finally, its adoption by a particular community can have a significant impact on intergovernmental relationships within the region and state in which the community is located.

Of course, it should be noted at the outset that the actual impacts of the use of these ordinances will be different in each community that adopts them. The amount and type of comprehensive planning undertaken, the underlying densities planned, the specific capital improvement schedules adopted, and the general application and administration of the ordinance—all of these have a direct bearing on its impacts and each will vary from community to community. In fact, the dissent in the Golden case in many respects went more to the application of the ordinance in Ramapo than to the validity of the ordinance itself.[91]

### Temporal Impacts

That the rate of development is affected in an area in which an adequate public facilities ordinance is adopted is obvious. The primary effect of the ordinance is explicitly to tie the rate of transition of land from rural to urban uses to the availability of urban services. The ordinance itself prohibits any intensive development until the requisite services are in place. The accompanying capital improvement schedule sets the time at which those services will be provided.

Use of the ordinance can have the effect of evening out developmental spurts and channeling development into a steady, balanced stream. Further, since decisions on the rate of urban development have been shifted from private to public hands, the community can more accurately and effectively program the provision of essential urban services. The community is placed in a situation in which it can act affirmatively in this area, rather than having to react continually to uncontrolled development.

Spatial Impacts

While an adequate public facilities ordinance in and of itself does not control the spatial character of development, it can be used to enforce a density pattern which is determined by the size of the proposed public facilities set out in the capital improvements schedule.[92] In this way, the ordinance is generally used to encourage urban infilling, by requiring that future development take the form of extensions of existing urban areas, to be served by incremental expansion of existing public facilities.[93]

Some observers contend that this implies a "continued extension of the status quo" and as such, makes city planning "little more than the translation of basic principles of civil engineering into suggested guidelines for development that minimize the costs of public facilities.[94] Indeed, if the adequate public facilities ordinance is based on a comprehensive plan which contemplates a continuous spread of low-density housing on large lots, it does serve, so to speak, to program urban sprawl.[95] This has been the charge leveled at the application of the ordinance in Ramapo. However, the plan can be used to encourage higher density levels, by, for example, providing sufficient services to and otherwise encouraging multi-family housing.

While the ordinance may or may not encourage continued urban spread, it is explicitly designed to prevent a second component of urban sprawl—"leapfrogging." This is the "pattern of development stimulated by the private market preference to develop land which costs less because it is furthest from supportive facilities, leaving large tracts of more expensive land undeveloped closer to serviced areas."[96] As a general rule, the adequate public facilities ordinance prevents this effectively. However, where the jurisdiction enacting the ordinance is too small, leapfrogging may actually be encouraged as developers will simply move beyond the reach of the ordinance and build their projects in uncontrolled areas. Thus a regional approach to the timing of development is necessary to make the use of these ordinances fully effective.

Environmental Impacts

The adequate public facilities ordinance can be used to further environmental objectives in several important ways. Its primary impact in this respect is to halt the problems caused by premature development. Without the ordinance, for example, rather intensive residential development could take place in an area unsuited for septic tanks, yet still unserved by water and sewer utilities. Then, if the septic tanks provided proved to be insufficient to handle the wastes generated, the community would be faced with the choice of either providing expensive utility services before it was ready, and without reference to a capital improvements program, or of allowing serious environmental damage to continue. Unfortunately, the fiscal condition of many localities would preclude the former choice, and thus the community and the affected homeowners would be forced to suffer increasing levels of ground water pollution. It is often only when the physical health of the community is actually endangered that ameliorative action is undertaken.

The adequate public facilities ordinance can also be used to steer development away from environmentally sensitive areas. This is accomplished simply by not providing urban services in those areas. A capital improvements program with this objective would be designed so as to encourage urban development at a rational pace, and only in those areas best suited for it. Services would not, for example, be extended to conservation or agricultural production areas.

### Economic Impacts

The adequate public facilities ordinance can have several positive economic effects for the jurisdiction adopting it. First, by allowing development to take place only as services are provided, a capital improvements program can be adopted which will provide services in the most economical way possible. This enables the community to defer the large capital expenditures which would have accompanied more rapid growth.

Another positive economic impact of the ordinance is the reduction of speculation in the private land market. Unlike the use of excessively large minimum lot size requirements to establish holding zones, an adequate public facilities ordinance of the type adopted in Ramapo makes definite the eventual use and density classification for each parcel of land in the community.[97] If variances in the prescribed schedule are granted only upon actual fulfillment of rigid preset conditions (that is, if the developer provides the necessary level of services himself), then everyone in the community can tell, with a high degree of certainty, both to what uses a particular parcel can be put and when that development can take place. This assurance could help stabilize land costs in developing areas, and certainly would do so in protected and conservation areas, by reducing speculation in the private land market.

The adequate public facilities ordinance cannot, however, be instituted without adverse economic impact. First, it may result in reduced tax revenues for the locality adopting it. Because ad valorem tax valuations are affected by the market value of the land, when substantial areas lose value because they are made at least temporarily undevelopable, tax revenues will fall. While this tax loss may in part

be made up by increased valuations on developable land, the community will in all probability be forced to look to the savings gained
through the more economical provision of urban services to make up
for the loss entirely. If these gains are as large as is usually anticipated, the lost tax revenue will indeed be a small price to pay.[98]

A more serious adverse economic impact is the effect of the ordinance on land costs in the community. If sizable tracts of land are
effectively removed from the development market—and it is estimated
that in Ramapo at least half of the previously developable land was[99]—
it can be assumed that the law of supply and demand will push the cost
of developable land up as competition among developers for potential
development sites increases.[100] Unless other ameliorative action is
undertaken, such as allowing increased densities in the developable
area, the effect of the ordinance will be to raise housing costs substantially.

One potential way of dealing with these increased costs is to
use the development timing ordinance to further a land banking strategy.[101] This assumes that the community could purchase, at low
cost, land that is currently in private hands but which could not be
developed for long periods of time. This land would eventually be used
to provide lower-income housing, thus lowering overall housing
costs. This, however, is a long-term solution and does not alleviate
the immediate burden imposed on middle- and lower-income families
by higher housing costs.

Social Impacts

One of the primary drawbacks to the use of the adequate public
facilities ordinance is adverse social impact caused by the above-
mentioned rise in housing costs. Indeed, if the capital improvement
plan underlying the ordinance is designed to support only low-density
housing, and the community undertakes no efforts to assume its fair
share of the regional housing load, the ordinance can properly be
labelled an exclusionary device.

The application of the ordinance in Ramapo has been attacked by
a number of observers on just such grounds.[102] There, the town made
virtually no provision for multi-family dwellings and required large
minimum lot sizes for single-family units. The result, when combined
with restrictions on the supply of developable land, was an estimated
minimum new house cost of $40,000 to $45,000.[103]

Such high housing costs, even if not the result of an exclusionary
intent, can insure the continued residential segregation of class and
racial groups. In the Golden case, the provision of approximately 200
units of low-income housing, 150 of which were reserved for the
elderly, was held by the court to be sufficient action for the ameliora-

tion of these exclusionary impacts. Fewer than ten black families were housed in these projects.[104] And this is in a rapidly growing suburb of New York City! If all other New York suburbs adopted development restrictions modeled after the Ramapo plan, with similar token acceptance of low-income housing, the resultant racial and economic segregation would be obvious, and quite unacceptable.

Another of the potential adverse social impacts of these ordinances is a possible loss of jobs, and even a general economic turndown, which could result if growth in the community were significantly slower. The seriousness of this potential effect will, of course, vary greatly from community to community. As most adequate public facilities ordinances will be directed towards managing growth, as opposed to stopping or even severely limiting it, this factor may well not create any problems in most communities.

Impact on Intergovernmental Relations

Given the new and growing state interest in planning and control of development, it would be counterproductive for local governments to be given this new power carte blanche. This feeling placed a large part in the dissenting opinion filed in the Golden case.[105] There it was contended that any such new powers, because of the impact on state and regional planning, should only be given to localities by the state legislature through an express statutory grant. Such a course of action would allow the state to set standards, and criteria, and to otherwise control the use of this planning tool by localities.

The state control ordinance most frequently called for is some action designed to assure a regional approach to its use. Local governments are naturally primarily concerned with the local costs and revenues generated by growth. However, as they attempt to minimize costs and taxes for their citizens, they may well be imposing costs on the taxpayers of other localities or on the state as a whole.[106] However, if application of the ordinance is made only with a regional perspective, many of these tendencies can be overcome. For example, acceptance of a fair share of the regional low-income housing needs could be imposed as a precondition to allowing a locality to use an adequate public facilities ordinance, thereby assuring that the ordinance would not be used for exclusionary purposes. Further, greater regional cooperation among localities can prevent the problems caused by developers leapfrogging to outlying uncontrolled areas, as they do when a single locality adopts an adequate public facilities ordinance, thus making it less likely that the ordinance will add to the problem of "megalopolitan sprawl."[107] In addition, a cooperative regional approach would make possible the use of a greater level of

expertise in planning and administering the ordinance than many small
localities with significant areas of vacant land would be able to afford
if they were acting alone.

## DEVELOPMENT MORATORIA

One of the most direct means to retard either particular types
of growth or the development process in general is to block development at a key point. Known as development moratoria, this technique
has been put into use in many parts of the country. If urban growth
can be thought of as a land conversion process, conditions on its pro-
gress can be imposed at multiple levels of government.

### Purposes of Moratoria

Generally, development moratoria have been instituted to stop
or slow the conversion of land within a jurisdiction. Most have been
justified on the grounds that further development cannot be supported
by existing public services, and that unrestrained growth would seriously impair community health and safety. These growth restraints
have been exercised with an air of urgency. Some have been proposed
as interim development controls, in order to give the municipality
breathing space in which to enact a new comprehensive growth plan
or to fix population "caps." Concern over growing congestion and a
proper fear of dire environmental consequences lie behind the current
movement toward moratoria. The related problem of financing municipal service improvements is implicit in this trend.

### Levels of Government Applying Moratorium Techniques

The three levels of government—federal, state, and local—have
to varying degrees been involved in the imposition of moratoria. A
federal court upheld the federal government when, through the Environmental Protection Agency (EPA), it blocked the issuance of building permits for new construction in Douglas County, Nevada, until
facilities for water treatment, approved by the state, and supported
by EPA, were built.[108] A statutory authority for such action does
exist and local groups in Washington, D.C., have sought an EPA ban

on sewer hookups pursuant to Section 402 (h) of the Federal Water Pollution Control Act.[109] It remains to be seen whether EPA will further
inject itself into the growth control movement by means of the moratorium power.

On the state level, sewer moratoria have been imposed upon
communities by thirteen state governments: Connecticut, New Hamp-
shire, Pennsylvania, Massachusetts, New Jersey, Maryland, West
Virginia, Tennessee, Ohio, Oklahoma, Iowa, California, and Oregon.[110]
This action has usually been taken to enforce state water quality
standards. For instance, the New Jersey Department of Environmental
Protection has placed construction moratoria on twenty-six local governments because their sewer treatment facilities had reached or exceeded capacity.[111] In a similar action, the Pennsylvania Department
of Environmental Resources issued a construction ban for municipalities with overloaded sewer capacities.[112] This moratorium can only
be lifted when the treatment capacities reach a level equal to present
and projected levels of demand for waste treatment. The Ohio Environmental Protection Agency prohibited sewer line extensions in the
Dayton area until county officials improved operations at the two
treatment facilities serving the region.[113] And finally, the Hawaii
State Legislature is considering legislation to impose a one-year
moratorium on the zoning of agricultural land.[114]

Moratorium techniques are used most commonly by local government, including town, city, and county elected officials, zoning
boards, and special service commissions. Occasionally such action
is taken pursuant to a public vote or referendum. From all indications, the development moratorium is being used, in one form or another, in hundreds of localities throughout the nation. The range of
moratorium type is great. How these types are distributed will be
discussed in a later portion of this section. Most local moratorium
activity is legally founded in the delegated grant of the police power
from the state constitution. Since many moratoria are relatively
short-term actions, and since on their face they are directed toward
the preservation of public health and welfare, the courts have generally looked upon them favorably.


Time Frame for Moratoria


The duration of development moratoria has been the focus of
considerable attention from interested municipalities, developers,
and property owners. The time element exposes the planning technique to the traditional legal attacks of public taking and unreasonableness of regulation. While some judicially recognized upper limit

to the length of moratoria seems to be assumed by many observers, time limits are in fact not at all well defined. Even carefully limited moratoria are not immune to successful judicial challenge. A New Jersey court found that a three and one-half year moratorium on apartment construction was excessively long, and struck it down.[115] The following examples exhibit the range of moratorium lengths that have been used in several localities. In Charlottesville, Virginia, sewer hookups within a one-mile radius of the town have been prohibited for a year and a half so that a treatment facility can be completed.[116] In Long Beach, New York, a six-month moratorium on all major building projects was enacted to allow time to develop a new zoning ordinance.[117] Hialeah, Florida took the same action for similar reasons but only for a period of ninety days.[118] West St. Paul, Minnesota, Florence Township, New Jersey,[119] and West Amwell Township, New Jersey,[120] have instituted moratoria for one hundred and twenty days, six months, and eighteen months, respectively, each for the purpose of revising their comprehensive or master plans. Finally, Elmwood Park, New Jersey,[121] passed a moratorium on building within the flood plain to last until the town had time to construct a plan for the area. The time limits are intended to be sufficient to allow the needed action to be taken, but it is clear that there is no consensus as to the fixing of permissible limits. Administrative and judicial decisions have been made on the basis of a case-by-case analysis, giving due consideration to local conditions. Consequently it is not possible to identify permissible time limits for various types of moratoria.

In June, 1973, the Department of Housing and Urban Development (HUD) surveyed their area offices specifically on the subject of the existence of sewer moratoria in each jurisdiction.[122] The responses identified 226 areas as employing sewer moratoria in one form or another. The results showed that at the time of the survey: 28 percent had had sewer bans in existence for less than six months, 40 percent had had them for periods of six months to a year, 12 percent had had them for one to two years, and 15 percent had them for more than two years.[123] The remaining 6 percent did not know what the time length was or did not have the information available. This data indicates the recent emergence of sewer moratoria as a major growth control technique. Interestingly, approximately two-thirds of those jurisdictions identified by the HUD survey voiced an intention to continue their moratoria for long or indefinite periods of time.[124]

Distribution of Moratoria Throughout the Country

One of the few available surveys directed at finding regional trends was prepared by the International City Management Association (ICMA) in the spring of 1973 and was distributed to 2,921 cities and counties in the United States.[125] Responses were received from 1,292 cities and counties, a 44 percent response rate. The ICMA questionnaire asked whether local moratoria had been imposed for environmental reasons in the past two years. Overall 203 cities and 33 counties, representing 18 percent of those responding, stated that moratoria were being used.[126] Of the 203 cities that reported imposing moratoria in the past two years, 63.5 percent were suburban. While areas in western states have used moratoria more frequently, the survey indicates the active use of this technique in all regions: Northeast, 18 percent; North Central, 15 percent; South, 15 percent; and West, 27 percent.[127] In contrast, the HUD survey of sewer moratoria (referred to above) reported that the bulk of actions were occurring primarily in three areas: South Florida (Miami, Tampa, and St. Petersburg), Cleveland, and northern New Jersey.[128]

Survey Results


        The survey instrument prepared by the research team, which is fully reported in Chapter 4, included questions regarding the use of various forms of moratoria for the management of growth. The five moratorium variations examined included moratoria on building permit issuance, water and sewer extension, water and sewer hookup, subdivision approval, and zoning changes. Most respondents replied to the inquiries regarding the use of moratoria; the response rate never fell below 90 percent on these questions. The frequency of use pattern among the 25 percent that reported using moratoria was as follows: 44 percent used building permit moratoria, 51 percent used water and sewer extension moratoria, 36 percent used water and sewer hookup moratoria, 25 percent used subdivision moratoria, and 41 percent used legislative zoning change moratoria. This presents a markedly uniform picture of an acceptance of all techniques except for subdivision moratoria.
        A second section of the questionnaire attempted to evaluate the effectiveness of each of the five moratoria. In general, there was a much lower response rate for the evaluative portion of the survey than for the informational part. This is not surprising, since only those respondents with experience in the use of the techniques would be able to comment upon their effectiveness. Those answering rated specific tools as very or moderately effective in the following proportions: 81 percent so rated building permit moratoria, 90 percent so rated water/sewer extension moratoria, 100 percent so rated water/sewer hookup moratoria, 88 percent so rated subdivision moratoria, and 68 percent so rated legislative zoning change moratoria.

The survey underlines the fact that moratoria of various types are being employed by a substantial number of governmental units throughout the country. However, moratoria are not isolated from the overall perspective of planning future growth. Moratoria involving water and sewer utility policy are most frequently and effectively used as growth timing devices. This is consistent with the trend in development timing ordinances of linking future growth with the expansion of urban services, an approach which has received judicial approval in Golden v. Planning Board of the Township of Ramapo (1972) from the New York Court of Appeals, the state's highest court.[129]

The finding that the subdivision approval moratorium is the least used of all of the five moratorium techniques presents an enigma, since subdivision approval would appear to provide a very effective and appropriate control over large scale development. Only twenty percent indicated its present operation and seventy-eight percent stated unequivocally that they did not use such a control and did not intend to do so in the future.

## Development Moratoria: A Definition and Classification

The land development process can be best characterized as a complex series of actions and interactions, by and between private and public actors, resulting in a more intensive use of land. Various legal requisites must be met before a private (or public) developer can construct buildings on land. Recognizing that these legal and administrative requirements are necessary conditions precedent to land conversion, governmental officials have attempted to manipulate them in order to slow growth or stop it altogether. Moreover, local officials have been quick to realize the extent of their power.

In surveying the literature, we have found that moratoria have been imposed on many different points of the development process, and that it is not uncommon for one municipality to be using several types of moratorium at once. The ICMA study revealed that in the 236 localities reporting the use of moratoria, 355 devices were employed.[130] This average of 1.5 moratoria in each locality reveals the great dispersion of the technique and its widespread multiple use.

Development moratoria presently being used in the nation can be classified according to the process they affect: (1) building permit issuance; (2) sanitary sewer facility extension (trunk lines); (3) sanitary sewer hookup to existing facilities; (4) legislative rezoning (amendment to ordinance or master plan); (5) administrative zoning changes (special or conditional use permits, variances, and so on); (6) subdivision regulations; (7) water facility extension (trunk lines and pumping stations); (8) water hookup to existing facilities; (9) natural gas line connections; (10) building on coastal land; and some (11) are general proclamations curbing construction. The moratoria are administered and initiated by different actors in different communities (for example, the zoning board, the planning board, sewer and water commissioners, the town council, citizens acting through referenda, and so on). Control of residential development has been the target of most moratoria, and high-density residential construction has received special attention. Each type of moratorium identified deserves closer scrutiny.

## Building Permits

The cessation of the issuance of building permits is a common and direct method of stopping construction. Building permits are legal requirements for construction in most areas. Randallstown, Maryland,[131] Tallahassee, Florida,[132] Baltimore County, Maryland,[133] Stonington, Connecticut,[134] and Douglas County, Nevada[135] all have prohibited the granting of building permits for varying lengths of time. Such a moratorium can be imposed after an official proclamation or by informal administrative decision.

## Sewer/Water Extension

A freeze on sewer extension has been attempted in several places. This entails the withholding of authorization for the extension of sewer trunk lines into areas which are presently unsewered. This growth guidance tool is quite effective in areas in which local authorities can influence capital expenditure decisions over a substantial period of time, and in which septic tanks cannot be used. That the legality of this technique is more likely to be upheld if there is a direct relationship between growth guidance and capital investment policies has been underscored in the recent cases involving adequate public facilities ordinances (those of Ramapo, New York, and Fairfax County, Virginia). Regional effect can be an equally important factor. Most moratoria have been independent acts of individual local entities, and can be used in unorganized ways, sometimes causing harm to the region as a whole.

## Sewer/Water Hookup

The sewer hookup freeze has been the most prevalent of moratoria, largely because local governments can more effectively control the connection process to existing sewage facilities. Such an action serves to prohibit the connection of buildings to an existing trunk line.

Charlottesville, Virginia,[136] Cobb County, Georgia,[137] Newark, Delaware,[138] Bordentown County, New Jersey,[139] and Montgomery County, Maryland[140] have all adopted this method of discouraging growth in certain areas, at least temporarily. Usually control of the permit issuance system for sewer connections can implement this form of regulation.

## Legislative Rezoning

Some areas have prohibited legislative amendment of their zoning ordinances until thorough studies can be undertaken to evaluate the effect that the revision would have on the local comprehensive or master plan. The justification for slowing the procedure for obtaining changes in the zoning ordinance is that use classifications should be altered only after a total development plan has been prepared. The Hawaiian state legislature considered three bills in 1973 which would have imposed rezoning moratoria on conversion of agricultural land to other use for one year.[141] Hialeah, Florida enacted a ninety-day ban on zoning changes for undeveloped land to prevent conversion, and to make possible a revision of the local zoning ordinance.[142]

## Administrative Zoning Changes

Administrative zoning changes have also been manipulated in order to slow development pressures. Special or conditional use permits for high-density residential construction have been withheld. For instance, Alameda, California has instituted an apartment moratorium to freeze the number of apartment units at its present level.[143] Some localities have gone even further by passing ordinances which seek to ban high rise apartments altogether (for example, Coral Gables, Florida[144]). Ocean City, Maryland is considering the imposition of height limitations.[145] Some areas have refused to grant permits for building on or near flood plains and for the construction of mobile home parks, pending various types of further study. The controlled administration or nonadministration of the zoning ordinance appears to be an attractive, short-term growth control measure.

## Subdivision Regulations

Some municipalities have tried to prevent the large-scale development which a subdivision creates by establishing moratoria on the operation of subdivision regulations. Harpswell, Maine has enacted a subdivision moratorium,[146] while West Amwell Township, New Jersey has recently voted to stop subdivision approvals for six months.[147] Ada County, Idaho, fearful that its agricultural land would be rapidly developed, has prohibited all subdivision on agricultural land and has placed it in a holding zone with a five-acre minimum lot requirement.[148] In many areas the size of proposed or potential subdivisions and the demands they would place on local services make it imperative that local governments enact moratoria.

## Water Service Extension

Water supply, like sewer services, is vital to residential growth. Some jurisdictions have manipulated this lever on growth management in much the same way that they have controlled sewer extension and sewer hookup policy. In Marin County, California, the local water commission prohibited the issuance of new building permits for a substantial part of the county, on the ground that the water system could not support an increased demand.[149]

## Natural Gas Line Connections

The distribution of natural gas has been used as a growth control technique in at least one locality. In Colorado Springs, Colorado, the city supplies natural gas as a public utility. The city, maintaining that it cannot supply gas to new homes, has established a fourteen-month moratorium on gas hookups.[150] While the reason for this type of development moratorium might be directly related to the present energy crisis, the technique does effectively slow residential construction in areas where home heating is provided primarily by gas.

## Building on Coastal Land

Several state-wide coastal zone regulations have been enacted which could slow or stop various kinds of development. The Delaware Coastal Zone Act of 1971 prohibits industrial construction within a defined coastal area.[151] California passed, through a voter initiative, a coastal protection law which requires special permits for all building within one thousand yards of the shore.[152] Several other states have contemplated such action. Coastal zone management laws could be employed as a timing mechanism if sufficient legislative authority existed.

## General Construction Ban

A common local response to rapid growth has been the general construction ban. This device, issued under varying and sometimes questionable authority, does not use any particular regulatory system as a framework for enforcement. The local governmental unit merely

decrees that there will not be any building in general or of a specific
type for a specific period of time.

## Summary

This is a sample of the types of moratoria that are currently
being used. The discussion has not included any comment on their legality (since that will come later). In general terms, the moratorium
is receiving increasing attention and use, not as a cure for uncontrolled growth, but as a temporary delaying instrument. In the next
section, we will investigate the question of whether moratoria actually
serve that purpose.

## Observed and Projected Effects of Moratoria

## Environmental Quality

Most moratoria, in one way or another, are imposed to preserve
and/or improve environmental quality. Moratoria have been responses
to a perceived physical problem: unmanageable residuals generation.
The common thread in these diverse techniques is the fear that continued development will overwhelm natural environmental systems and
will make the task of future reclamation costly, if not impossible. Regardless of whether or not development moratoria have appreciably
slowed or stopped growth in the areas where they have been enacted
(and there is evidence to the contrary), the question of how well they
have served their environmental purpose is important.

There may have been relief from spiraling pollution in some
cases, but it must be remembered that the moratoria usually are relatively short. Implied in their institution is the building of greater pollution treatment capacity, or the production of an updated comprehensive development plan. The moratoria themselves provide only a
period of restraint before the inevitable expansion. Moratoria give
the locality or region a chance to plan for and perhaps influence development that is sure to occur. Funds or financing mechanisms can
be assembled for capital investment to support increased services.

Since moratoria are acts of independent jurisdictions, they relate poorly to regional approaches to environmental and growth problems. In fact, by their nature, local actions resist comprehensive
planning efforts. Because of this, moratoria can represent wrong responses to the right environmental issues.

Housing and Urban Development

Given that this control is so new that it has not been thoroughly evaluated, we address ourselves to whether or not development moratoria have, in fact, stopped or slowed growth. Some observers have argued that short-term moratoria have not reduced building activity, since the various governmental approvals necessary for construction are often procured well in advance. F. Lee Ruck, Fairfax, Virginia County Attorney, has estimated that 30,000 building permits are outstanding in his county in spite of its eighteen-month moratorium on building approval.[153] Consequently, the developer, and especially the large developer, is not impeded. Consultant Malcolm Rivkin has claimed that moratoria have accidentally accelerated development.[154] He argues that developers, knowing of an impending moratorium, and fearing the imposition of highly restrictive land use controls when it ends, will acquire a greater number of construction approvals than are presently needed as a hedge against the future. This will increase building activity even during the moratorium.[155]

But assuming that the moratorium is at least partially effective in reducing building opportunities, what are its secondary impacts? First, there is the possibility that housing starts will be shifted to other jurisdictions without moratoria. Moratorium imposition is an unorganized process; adjoining municipalities will not necessarily enact moratoria. As a result, housing demand for general area will simply shift to the locality without the control ordinance. The HUD survey asked whether or not housing starts were shifted due to moratoria.[156] The results from 220 responses are as follows:

| Category | Number | Percent |
|----------|--------|---------|
| None     | 18     | 8       |
| Little   | 127    | 58      |
| Moderate | 59     | 27      |
| Major    | 16     | 8       |

More than one-third of the answers found a moderate or major shift in housing starts due to a moratorium. Large-scale shifts could result in the formation of urban sprawl development patterns (with all their disadvantages) in adjacent jurisdictions that do not have moratoria. Such leapfrogging would subvert the notion of orderly development in that region, and could cause additional environmental degradation through an uncontrollable spurt in building.

Secondly, moratoria tend to raise the cost of existing housing by restricting the supply of housing on the market. No (or little) new housing is built, and the price of that which is constructed must include the inflated land cost. New housing reflects the high price level of the existing housing supply. The locality may rapidly become exclusive, and access to it limited. Even though people of other (lower) income groups may be employed in the town and may wish to live where they work, housing opportunities are effectively denied them. Some critics of the moratorium technique have asserted that moratoria, ostensibly based on environmental considerations, are surreptitious attempts at income and racial segregation. Moratoria prohibiting higher-density residential land uses (such as, apartments or townhouses) would undoubtedly have the effect of decreasing housing opportunities for those families with limited incomes. The result of the moratorium strategy with regard to those families with less than middle- or upper-middle incomes might be to concentrate them in central city areas. This would be especially true for racial minority groups.

Third, one positive ramification of the randomly disbursed, suburb-oriented moratorium strategy could be the development of previously undesirable land in the urban and suburban area. This has been identified as an ''infilling'' process, by which underutilized services are more efficiently consumed and the previously existing sprawl effect is improved. Here again, an appreciation of land value would accompany the development.

Finally, the moratorium strategy can have a substantial effect on the building industry. Small firms may be put out of business by moratoria. They cannot transfer operations to another area and do not have the finances to exist until the moratorium is lifted. The large construction firms are not restricted by these limitations and consequently are not detrimentally affected by the moratorium. Large firms also have the ability to anticipate moratoria and to hedge against their restrictions. Consequently, the burden of a development moratorium is inequitably placed on the small building company.

## The Future of Moratoria

Moratoria generally have not been overturned by the courts when they have been directed to the solution of easily identifiable and quantifiable problems. When a municipality has a well-known sewage disposal problem, the courts will probably not be anxious to invalidate a moratorium imposed to allow time for construction of a treatment facility. Of course, the moratorium, like any regulation, must be reasonably related to the attainment of a valid public purpose. But the moratorium can serve only a limited purpose. A moratorium responding to a local perception of overpopulation might not be so warmly received. For example, a federal district court ruled that

Petaluma, California may not limit population size through the use of a population "cap" since that would constitute an unconstitutional restriction of the right to travel.[157] However, since many moratoria have a short duration, any concerted legal effort to invalidate them would be futile.

Viewing the development moratorium in light of the managed growth concept, the technique is clearly limited. Many localities, seeking a simple answer to an immediate problem, seize upon moratoria and fail to investigate the underlying sources of growth pressure. The technique must be used as only one part of a comprehensive system of developmental regulation. Fairfax County, Virginia, in its Interim Development Ordinance, has attempted such an approach.[158] There, a building approval moratorium (lasting for eighteen months) serves as an introductory phase of a three-tiered plan that coordinates municipal service provision and county developmental planning. Moratoria can be effective managed-growth techniques only if they are utilized wisely, and not in a short-sighted, arbitrary fashion.


LAND BANKING


There is a growing recognition that effective development timing cannot be achieved by reliance solely upon growth management tools associated with the police power.[159] There are indications that government may have to take a more active role in the development process in order to have any significant impact on the pace of urban development. Several recent presidential and congressional reports have recommended a shift to positive programs of land acquisition and disposition. The Douglas Commission, for example, concluded that governments should obtain land through purchase in order to achieve land use objectives, and also recommended that state governments enact legislation enabling both state and local development authorities to acquire land in advance of development to insure the continuing availability of sites; control the timing, location, type, and scale of development; prevent urban sprawl; and reserve for the public those gains in land values resulting from governmental activity.[160] A similar recommendation for land banking has been proposed by the President's Committee on Urban Housing.[161]

Land banking, which is the public acquisition and holding of undeveloped land in anticipation of either future public use or resale in order to accomplish community goals, can be initiated to serve either one or both of its basic purposes. The first purpose is to acquire sites for future public facilities in advance of actual need. The second purpose is to use public ownership of undeveloped land to influence the character and timing of future community growth. There are important conceptual and pragmatic differences between these two purposes of land banking. For the first purpose, early site acquisition, a shorter time horizon, and less acquisition of vacant land are involved. Also, land purchases are limited to areas of future expansion of public facilities. Land banking for the purpose of managing community growth implies a long-range program of public acquisition of large amounts of land in developing urban areas, generally to be held until the community determines that the area is ripe for urban development. The land can then be sold or leased for private use. In this way, the development decision is placed directly in public hands.

## Types of Land Banks

### Early Site Acquisition Land Banks

A 1966 survey conducted by the Institute of Public Administration revealed that approximately one-third of American cities with 50,000 or more inhabitants had early site acquisition programs.[162] In general, these acquisitions have been devoted to acquiring land for future public services such as schools, fire stations, libraries, neighborhood parks, airports, and highways. By purchasing land in anticipation of actual need, state and local governments have been able to (1) forestall rising prices caused by inflation, and (2) preempt private developers from developing those sites best suited for public use.

Montgomery County School Site Advanced Acquisition Program. Since 1955, the Board of Education of Montgomery County, Maryland, has been acquiring land in anticipation of future school needs.[163] The program requires the Division of Planning of the Department of School Facilities to estimate future pupil enrollment. These estimates are derived from the county's master plan and zoning ordinances. After determining the expected growth pattern of school enrollment, the timing of future sites is then determined by monitoring building permits, telephone connections, and the path of future public improvements. Finally, engineering site studies are made of specific sites.

The recommendations of the Department of School Facilities are reviewed by a Site Selection Advisory Committee, who in turn make their recommendations to the Montgomery County Board of Education. The Montgomery County Board of Education has the final authority for determining early site acquisitions. If the board decides to purchase the site, funds are obtained from its future site account.

This account is funded by the county's annual capital budget appropriation. Since the county appropriation process and the board's decisions on acquisition expenditures are independent, the future site program must await county appropriations. An important disadvantage of this annual appropriation procedure is the inability of the board of education to enter installment purchases or option agreements for future sites, because it cannot legally commit funds not yet appropriated. Moreover, yearly appropriations have shortened the holding period of land acquisitions. Thus, in 1966 fully 65 percent of the school sites acquired by the Montgomery County program were acquired less than five years in advance of anticipated need.[164]

Despite these limitations, a HUD-financed cost-benefit analysis of the Montgomery County Program concluded that "The program . . . has been of substantial net benefit to Montgomery County. Better sites have been acquired at lower costs than would otherwise be possible."[165]

Moreover, the average net benefit (at a six percent discount rate) for each of the seventeen sites surveyed was $37,000.[166]

Richmond, Virginia Early Land Acquisition Program. Richmond, Virginia has an early land acquisition program which allows the city to acquire property whenever private construction is contemplated on a parcel of land which has already been designated in the city master plan for some public use.[167] The Richmond program is designed to block new construction on sites scheduled for later public acquisition; it has allowed the city to avoid the need to purchase and demolish recently constructed improvements.

The Richmond Program requires the Commissioner of Buildings to notify the City Planning Commission of contemplated property improvements on property set aside in the city master plan for future use, and to delay for thirty days the granting of a building permit. If the City Planning Commission decides to purchase the property, the permit is further delayed until the City Council approves the acquisition.

A HUD cost-benefit evaluation of the Richmond advance acquisition program revealed a benefit-cost ratio of 2:1.[168]

State and Regional Projects. In addition to early public service site acquisition, early site acquisition programs have been used for highways,[169] public housing,[170] industrial parks,[171] airports,[172] and other state and regional development projects. In California, for example, a $30 million revolving fund has been used to finance early highway right of way acquisition. Between 1952 and 1966, California spent $62.5 million for early land purchases. Its Division of Highways has estimated that if the same properties had been acquired when

actually needed, the cost would have been $380.5 million.[173] Thus the
program, over a fourteen-year period, saved the state approximately
$318 million.

Summary. The California, Montgomery County, and Richmond early
acquisition programs have resulted in significant cost savings and,
probably, better sites. Moreover, early site acquisition programs are
applicable to both local and state development projects. However,
early site acquisitions programs may not be successful in all circumstances. Localities lacking comprehensive planning capabilities will
be unable to use land banking effectively. This is particularly significant because many of those areas presently experiencing rapid urban
growth are located in nonurban areas which have relatively weak planning capabilities. Furthermore, early site acquisition is most effective when institutional decision-making responsibilities are not frag-
mented among various local governments. In Montgomery County,
Maryland, a single board of education, planning commission, and
county council had the jurisdiction to educate, plan, and govern the
entire county. Within this governmental complex the broader issues
of urban growth could be considered together.[174] Such is not the situation in many areas of the country. Finally, although early site acquisition land banks have insured the availability of optimal sites for
future public use at current rather than future prices, they have had
little influence on the promotion of orderly land development.

## Land Banking to Manage Urban Growth

Despite the recent recommendations emphasizing public acquisition and the successes of early site acquisition programs, we were
unable to find any American jurisdiction, with the exception of Puerto
Rico, that has used public acquisition to explicitly control the timing
and location of urban growth.[175] Urban renewal programs, which are
somewhat analogous to the land banking programs under discussion
here, have been undertaken in many American communities. Under
these programs, with substantial federal financial aid, local communities acquired large tracts of land, usually located in deteriorating
central city areas. After the land was cleared, the normal procedure
was to resell it to private developers. So, while there was significant
public participation in the acquisition and assembly of these tracts,
there was no land banking in the sense of holding the tracts for publicly determined future use. However, public acquisition for land
banking to manage growth has been used in both Europe and Canada.

The preeminent example of public land banking for growth
management has been the development and expansion of Stockholm,
Sweden. Since 1904, Stockholm has had a policy of large scale land

purchases. Today it has more than eighteen planned communities, with a combined population of 250,000; more than half of the city's population lives in areas acquired by land banking.[176]

Similar examples of land banking are found in Edmonton and Saskatoon, in Canada.[177] Both cities adopted land banking plans to control rapid urban expansion. To achieve their objectives, Edmonton and Saskatoon each zoned part of its area for exclusive agricultural use, prohibited septic tanks, and initiated utility expansion programs. These controls encouraged development on city-acquired land. Consequently, by regulating the disposition of city-owned land, Edmonton and Saskatoon were able to affect the timing and location of urban growth. For example, during the past decade in Saskatoon, 80 percent of its residential and 95 percent of its industrial development has taken place on city-acquired property.[178]

Managed Growth Objective. Large public acquisitions permit public agencies to affect directly the timing and location of future development. Land banks, by acquiring large amounts of developable land, limit the supply of land. The government is then able to influence the timing and location of future development through the disposition of acquired lands.

Another advantage of land banking is its suitability for combatting urban sprawl. In the past, urban sprawl has been caused by land speculators who refuse to sell their property at prices deemed to be reasonable by developers. Unable to obtain this land at reasonable prices, developers are forced to purchase and develop more remote but less expensive lands. However, public land banks, utilizing their power of eminent domain, have prevented leapfrog development.[179] Arguably, similar results could accrue to private development if private developers were granted similar powers.[180]

Furthermore, land banking is not vulnerable to judicial challenges based on the taking issue, since compensation is paid to the landowner when government purchases a parcel of land. In other countries land banks have influenced the quality of new development; American efforts to control the quality of urban renewal projects have not succeeded. When quality controls were attached to the disposition of land, it was difficult to find buyers in the private sector willing to take on the higher costs of developing within these restrictions.[181] Inner-city urban renewal experiences, however, may not be analogous to land banks in urban developing areas.

Price Objective. During the postwar period, increasing population and income, combined with a limited supply of land, have caused the price of vacant land to increase rapidly. For example, the average cost for sites of new FHA-insured housing doubled between 1956 and

1966. This increase was five times greater than the general increase in the Consumer Price Index during the same period.[182] Moreover, during the same ten-year period, the ratio of vacant land cost to total developed property value has increased from 14.2 percent to 20.7 percent, for FHA housing. Because of this sharp rise, land banks have attempted to influence land prices, and in many instances have been quite successful. For example, in Edmonton, Canada, land banking has permitted the city to sell housing lots at one-half the price of lots available in the private market.[183]

Land banks influence land prices in two ways. First, public ownership insures an adequate supply of developable land, and thereby eliminates the contrived scarcities caused by land speculators. If land banks were to dispose of their property at prices below the going market rate, the competing, cheaper government land would put downward pressure on all land prices.[184] Second, acquisition of land well in advance of actual need also forestalls inflation.

Two arguments are advanced against the use of land banking to lower land costs. First, several studies have indicated that during the acquisition phase, land banks may actually exacerbate inflation by reducing the supply of land.[185] Secondly, when public agencies acquire land in advance of actual need, they must pay additional holding costs. Consequently, the extent to which land banks achieve lower land costs largely depends upon how high public holding costs are. Where cost savings have accrued, indirect subsidies, such as exemptions from local property taxes and lower interest charges for the public sector, have reduced holding costs vis-a-vis private holding costs.[186]

Equity Objective. The third general objective of large public acquisitions is the recovery of windfall gains emanating from public investments.[187] This objective is based on the assumption that much of the increase in land values derives from public decisions and capital expenditures related to that land, and that the public ought to reap the economic benefits of public action.

Although this concept is implicit in all land banking, Puerto Rico, Sweden, and the Netherlands have made it an integral part of their land policy.[188] In the United States, Montgomery County in Maryland[189] and the states of Wisconsin[190] and Massachusetts[191] have permitted public authorities to acquire land adjacent to proposed public facilities such as highway interchanges in order to capture land value increases caused by public improvement. This advantage has been an outgrowth of land banking and not a rationale for land banks. Direct changes in the capital gains tax structure could achieve the same effect.[192]

Conclusion. To some extent, the objectives of land banking are contra-
dictory. For example, when land banks dispose of their property to
manage growth, their land reserves will be reduced, and consequently
their ability to regulate land prices will be compromised. Similarly,
when land banks dispose of their land to reduce inflationary pressures,
their ability to time development will be seriously threatened.[193]
     An examination of the multiple objectives of large scale public
acquisition has revealed that many land banking benefits are gained
at the expense of hidden costs and subsidies. Appropriate governmental policies can allow private development to achieve comparable
results, with the developers bearing the burden of these hidden costs.
     Economic gains for the public have never been the primary
reason for adopting land banking, however. Land banks coordinate
development programs, subsidies, land acquisition, and tax policies,
within one institution. Moreover, where land banking has been used,
localities have been able to influence the timing and location of development. Finally, localities and states can select from among the
several objectives of land banking those deemed appropriate for their
particular situation. Areas with large amounts of agricultural land
may decide to acquire land for future needs; developing urban areas
may attempt to manage growth; and urban areas may only adopt early
site-acquisition programs.


## Constraints on Land Banking


     In this section, institutional, administrative, financial, and legal
constraints on land banking are considered. The section is not intended as a manual for establishing a land banking system but rather
as an exploration of the major issues involved in implementing a land
bank.

### The Land Bank Entity

     To accomplish managed growth objectives, public land banks
must have the financial and legal power to purchase or condemn land
throughout a broad geographical area.[194] They must be able to plan
for a metropolitan-wide or regional area. Thus, it is crucial to select
the appropriate agency to administer them.

Metropolitan-Wide Agency. The most appropriate area of focus for
achieving land banking objectives is the metropolitan region. In general, this approach is consistent with the regional thrust of recent

environmental legislation and court decisions. However, most metropolitan areas, lacking general-purpose governmental authority, and general-purpose taxing and eminent domain powers, are presently incapable of implementing land banks. Consolidating county and city governments, or expanding the power of A-95 regional organizations or councils of governments, may permit more metropolitan planning; but prospects are dim.

Municipal Corporation. A second alternative, enactment of enabling legislation to permit municipal corporations to land bank, has limited possibilities. Most municipalities do not have the fiscal resources necessary for large scale land banking.[195] In addition, municipalities generally lack the extraterritorial authority to land bank in developing urban regions, the area where land banking is most effective. Wisconsin legislation permits a city to acquire property both within and outside it,[196] but in many areas of the United States the political realities of the city-suburb relationship render this alternative unlikely.

State Agency. Most states already possess the legal authority to land bank, and in fact, in many states land banking has been used successfully for early highway right-of-way acquisitions. The states' advantage of greater financial resources is offset in many cases by constitutional debt limitations which restrict the states' ability to finance large-scale public acquisition.[197] Furthermore, state land banking to manage growth may inappropriately involve state governments in what are usually considered local concerns. The prospects for state land banking to manage urban growth are thus more limited than its already demonstrated usefulness for state development projects.

Public Purpose Corporation. Some commentators have concluded that the public purpose corporation is the only governmental entity that could effectively operate a land bank.[198] The corporation lacks an essential factor, however—public responsiveness and accountability. Its advantages include freedom from debt limitation, immunity from local property taxes, and broad discretionary powers. Land bank decisions such as locating growth and distributing cost savings are public decisions, but the primary legal responsibility of a public purpose corporation is to its bondholders. The example of the New York Port Authority, a public purpose corporation for metropolitan transportation activity, indicates that the resolution of this conflict usually favors the bondholders.

Furthermore, under this authority the basic necessity of developing a metropolitan-wide comprehensive plan is not faced. A public purpose corporation has only acquisition and disposition responsibilities; it has no mandate to pursue its objectives with a regional perspective. Even in the presence of a master plan, the public purpose corporation could face serious difficulties. Because of the substantial investments it must make, the corporation must have some guarantee of the continuing viability of that plan.[199] Such guarantees, however, would greatly limit the flexibility of local governments to respond to the changing needs and desires of the community.

Conclusions. The problem of developing an appropriate entity for land banking is related to the crucial issue of metropolitan-wide or regional planning and government. Land banking can operate most efficiently within the context of an effective regional plan, but existing types of institutions are ill-equipped for the task.

## Financing Land Banks

Financing land banks depends upon the scope of their general objectives. Montgomery County, Maryland, has been able to finance its early acquisition program by general appropriations.[200] Land banking for the purpose of managing growth would require financial aid from both federal and state governments. Moreover, public acquisition will, by its nature, reduce a community's tax base. Consequently, large-scale public acquisition may compromise the financial position of local governments that are heavily dependent upon property taxes.

The principal source of funding large-scale acquisitions is debt financing. If governmental action were taken to grant tax-exempt status to land bank bonds, reduced interest charges could lead to substantial savings. Even so, debt financing would require land banks to commit themselves to policies which would assure their long-run profitability. These policies directly conflict with the noninflationary objective of land banking.[201]

Furthermore, court decisions may require land banks to acquire land according to a public plan. Although this requirement would be similar to urban renewal plans, close adherence to a public plan would make the acquisition process more costly. To avoid these increased land prices, the Swedish government has allowed the city of Stockholm, through the establishment of dummy organizations, to acquire land before a specific plan has been adopted.[202] Thus, to some extent, financial considerations may conflict with citizen participation.[203] Recently, Puerto Rico[204] and New York State[205] enacted legislation which allows their governments to acquire property without compensating the owner for increased property values caused by proposed public acquisition. Thus land banks could reduce acquisition costs without compromising citizen participation.

Legal Issues

Although legal concerns affect both early site acquisition and
managed growth land banking programs, early site acquisition programs have not been seriously challenged. Unlike managed growth
land banks, early site acquisition programs acquire sites for specific
public uses such as schools, fire stations, and roads. Consequently,
legal challenges to early site acquisition relate to timing rather than
the purpose of the acquisition itself. The courts have generally upheld the right of localities to acquire land well in advance of actual
need.[206] For example, the North Carolina Supreme Court has held
that "if the taking is in reality for the purpose of making the property
available for use by the public, it is immaterial that, in the immediate
future, only a small segment of the public will be likely to make actual use of it."[207]
Although the constitutionality of early site acquisition programs
appears to be settled, the right of land banks to exercise the power
of eminent domain for the purpose of managing growth remains unde-
cided. If land banks have no condemnation power, land speculators
could refuse to sell their land and thereby frustrate managed growth
objectives. Thus, the vital legal question for managed growth land
banking is whether the control of urban growth in and of itself is a
public purpose.
Traditionally, the power of eminent domain was limited to land
that was intended for a specific public use, such as a fire station or
a school. However, this interpretation has been gradually expanded
to permit government acquisitions for a "public purpose." A public
purpose includes the police powers of public safety, health, and
morals. Urban renewal statutes have been upheld because slum
clearance protects public health and safety.[208] More recently, the
courts have taken a broader perspective on public purpose. The
United States Supreme Court, in Berman v. Parker, has indicated
that eminent domain could be applied to a much wider set of objectives than traditional police powers.[209] Following that decision, some
courts have allowed redevelopment agencies to condemn vacant land
in order to facilitate development.[210] More recently, the Supreme
Court of Puerto Rico, citing Berman v. Parker, has upheld the use
of eminent domain for land banking.[211] This decision has been the
only American court test of land banking. In conclusion, "the trend
of the modern court decisions show a continuing enlargement of the
scope of public purpose. . . . Given this trend it is likely that the
doctrine of public purpose will not constitute a significant road block
to use public land assembly to control the development on the fringes
of metropolitan areas."[212]

In addition to possible constitutional limitations, there are also statutory limitations. Since localities are created by the states, they derive all of their powers from the state. Consequently, before land banking programs are initiated, state enabling legislation must be enacted.

## Acquisition of Various Rights in Land

The decision as to the quantity of land a locality should purchase depends on its objectives. Land banking to manage growth requires more land acquisition than does future site acquisition. Finances also play a role. Alternative methods for acquiring land have differing consequences.

Fee Simple. If property rights are likened to a bundle of sticks, then fee simple is equivalent to owning all the sticks. A fee simple owner acquires immediate unrestricted ownership and possession of his property. The fee simple permits the maximum degree of control of land use. Despite the higher cost (unencumbered land comes at a higher price), fee simple acquisition for areas of immediate public development is probably the most appropriate form of acquisition.

Easements and Development Rights. With this approach, a public agency acquires a negative easement which restricts the owner from certain uses or alterations of his land. For example, government, through the acquisition of certain development rights, could prevent development of a specified nature from taking place on the property. The major advantage of this tool is economic. Moreover, the property in question is not removed from the tax rolls, and government does not have to make public outlays for maintenance. The Wisconsin Highway Commission has been acquiring scenic easements for a number of years. The cost of the acquisition of these rights has averaged approximately one-half the cost of comparable fee simple acquisitions.[213]
Despite cost savings, easements have not been widely used. First, in developing urban areas, the cost of easements which significantly restrict the use of the land approaches the cost of fee simple. Moreover, the administrative costs of acquiring and enforcing easements are high.

Life Estates. Public agencies willing to delay public occupancy for long periods of time can achieve substantial cost savings by purchasing a fee simple encumbered with a life tenancy. Under this arrangement public occupancy is delayed as the tenant retains rights of occupancy and use for the duration of his natural life. Life estates remove property from the tax rolls, but the acquisition expenditures and maintenance costs associated with them are lower.

Options. An option agreement permits a public agency to purchase property at its present market value but defers actual purchase until a later date. Of course, in developing urban areas, the cost of such options, particularly if they are of any substantial duration, are quite high. Landowners will refuse to tie up their holdings unless they receive substantial compensation.

Tax Delinquencies. Purchasing land at tax sales is another method for acquiring a fee simple interest. Legislation authorizing local governments to acquire tax-delinquent land is very common. Since 1959, Philadelphia has been acquiring tax-delinquent land for open spaces.[214] Jackson County, Missouri has established a land trust to manage land acquired through tax delinquency.[215] However, if land banks only were to acquire tax-delinquent properties, their ability to determine the location of acquisitions would be severely limited. Moreover, public purposes may not be best served by having public property scattered throughout various locations.[216]

### Interim Land Management Policies

During the period between acquisition and disposition, land banks have to manage their property. Various management tools are available, depending on the objectives of the land bank, and the length of the holding period. The most common interim device is leasing newly acquired land for uses which do not interfere with future development. These uses include agriculture, recreation, and wildlife preserves. Both Montgomery County, Maryland, and Richmond, Virginia[217] have leased land acquired under their early land-acquisition programs.

Interim land management also involves coordinating public ownership with community planning. This is particularly true when planning and acquisition are done by separate organizations. For example, when the state acquires land in anticipation of future highway construction, to what extent should the state's interim management of that land be restricted by local planning?

### Disposition

The major issues of disposition include its timing, location, price, and manner. If land banks did not undertake their own development programs, the disposition of publicly owned land could at least be timed to coincide with provision of public facilities. The land bank would simply hold the land until the level of public facilities allowed development. Furthermore, land banks could influence the quality of development by attaching development covenants to deeds. This technique has been used successfully in Rotterdam.[218] Finally, land banks could keep some land for future public uses such as schools, parks, and public housing.

Swedish land banks develop their own land, and upon completion of development, lease developed properties to the public. These leases contain restrictions on use and property, and are usually written so as to run for 40 to 74 years.[219] The major advantage of leasing is that it facilitates ultimate redevelopment and allows the locality to exercise greater control of existing use. However, leaseholders may lack the incentive to maintain their property, as the expiration date nears.[220]

Another major disposition issue, the price of disposed property, has serious implications. The choices are either to sell the property at present market value, or to sell it at some reduced price which would include purchase and holding costs, but would not necessarily be full market value. For example, by providing low-cost land to high-quality development programs, Canadian land banks have been able to induce a high quality of development. As already indicated, there exists a conflict between the land banks' financial viability and the provision of low-cost land for housing and open spaces. Moreover, if low-cost land is provided to developers, what will prevent them from making windfall profits? The Canadian land banks have placed stringent controls on private developers to prevent profiteering. For example, Red Deer, Alberta retains the title to land until the builder begins actual construction.[221] However, any disposition of land at prices lower than present market value should contain assurances that the land will be used as intended.

## Conclusions

An analysis of the major institutional, financial, legal and administrative issues surrounding land banking for both early site acquisition and growth management purposes has revealed that there are impediments to large-scale acquisition programs. But when associated with early site acquisition, these are not insurmountable. Given state aid such as guidance, encouragement, and appropriate enabling legislation, many localities can use land banking to reduce their land acquisition costs substantially. Moreover, land banking can help localities guide growth, by using early site acquisition to assure that an adequate supply to properly located sites for future expansion of public facilities will be available when needed.

Although the institutional, financial, and legal constraints are
more exacting for large-scale public acquisitions designed to accomplish growth management objectives, these problems are not insurmountable. Recent decisions indicate that the courts will be receptive
to community efforts aimed at growth management. The administrative tools already exist, for the most part, so the administration of
land banks is within present capabilities. The two greatest obstacles
to growth-management land banking are the lack of an institutional
framework for metropolitan-wide planning, and the problem of amas-
sing sufficient financial resources for large-scale land acquisition.


Disposition and Management of Public Lands


Nearly 39 percent of the nation's land is publicly owned.[222] Consequently, the disposition and management of public land can directly
affect managed growth efforts. The Public Law Review Commission
has recommended revision of federal law in a manner that would aid
orderly growth and development.[223] Failure to follow this policy
could have lasting environmental effects on nearby localities. Although typical uses of federal public land include grazing, timber har-
vesting, mineral production, and recreation, townsite laws authorize
land to be used for community development.[224] Moreover, surplus
federal lands have also been sold for community development.[225]
Managing public land involves conflicting interests. Decisions
affecting large tracts of public land influence the environment, employment prospects, and the growth of surrounding communities. For
example, federal policies allowing timbering in national forests have
encouraged lumbering concerns to locate in adjacent communities.
This economic advantage to the locality is offset by the soil erosion
and siltation of nearby streams brought on by timbering. Timbering
also precludes alternative uses of land, such as wildlife preserves
and recreation facilities. Therefore, the Public Land Law Review
Commission has proposed that dominant uses and compatible secondary uses be established for all federally owned land.[226] The commission felt that ad hoc administrative decision making unrelated to
land use planning did not provide sufficient guidance for federal investments and local planning.
It is also true that local activities can adversely affect the environment of public lands.[227] Therefore, the Public Land Law Review Commission has recommended that (1) all federal agencies be
required to submit their plans to state and local government agencies
for review; and (2) public agencies should acquire easements over

lands in nonfederal ownership when necessary to protect environmental values on public land.[228]

## TAXATION

Of the many guidance techniques identified in this study, few have as universal an impact on social and economic issues as does taxation policy.[229] Taxes have been imposed by various levels of government for essentially two purposes: the acquisition of revenues for governmental operation, and the regulation of social and economic activity. Revenue raising has been cited as the constitutionally permissible purpose for the the exercise of the power to tax, but in many cases, the facts show that the intended objective of the tax was regulation. The decisions of the United States Supreme Court have reflected its changing attitude toward the purposes of taxation in this century. In early cases, such as McGray v. United States[230] and Bailey v. Drexel Furniture,[231] the Court struck down a tax on child labor by stating that an interest in regulation and social policy could only be incidental to revenue collecting. But as time passed, various "incidental" purposes were allowed. In United States v. Kahriger,[232] a large tax on gambling activities was upheld, as was the high tax on the possession of dangerous armaments in United States v. Sonzinski.[233] It is apparent that the Supreme Court recognizes and accepts the role of taxation as a regulatory mechanism.

Traditionally, taxes have been imposed in three distinct fact situations: (1) on the earning of income, (2) on the purchase of goods and services, and (3) on the ownership of real property and improvements. Viewing the potential capabilities of the governmental power to tax, some observers have suggested that it be directed as a policy tool, along with other government actions, to influence developmental patterns and timing. Unfortunately, we have little empirical data to support assertions concerning the usefulness of the taxation mechanism as a land use control technique. Consequently, most proposals involving the manipulation of the tax power for this purpose have remained speculative. In this section, a description and evaluation of some current examples of taxation techniques that directly and indirectly affect development will be made. Also, we will examine the survey response from planners in the field on their view of the potential of tax policy as a growth management tool.

As an introductory caveat, it must be remembered that a governmental body's power to tax is circumscribed by its constitutional authority and the constitutional case law on the subject. First, a differential tax program might be open to attack as a violation of the

equal protection clause of the federal and state constitutions. Under
the traditional equal protection analysis, a tax may not be imposed
differently upon similarly situated individuals unless there is a reasonable basis for the distinction between taxpayers. If such a classification is suspect and infringes upon fundamental constitutional interests or rights, then the taxing body would have to justify its practice
by showing a compelling state interest. Second, state constitutions
usually specify the taxing authority of the locality within narrow
bounds and often require that assessment, valuation, and taxing practices be uniform throughout the state. For example, the North Carolina state constitution states that

> only the General Assembly shall have the power to clas-
> sify property for taxation, which power shall be exercised
> only on a state-wide basis and shall not be delegated. No
> class of property shall be taxed except by uniform rule,
> and every classification shall be made by general law uni-
> formly applicable in every county, city and town, and other
> unit of local government.[234]

Furthermore, the constitution provides that the power to tax shall only
be exercised for public purposes.[235] It would be necessary to determine whether growth management could be included under such a classification. In addition, the state of North Carolina has instituted a
policy of tax uniformity by requiring all counties to list their real
property at a uniform rate of one hundred percent of assessed or true
valuation.[236] These constitutional hurdles, and others found in other
state constitutions, must be considered when taxation is to be incorporated into a growth management strategy.


## Federal Tax Policy


The federal government is the nation's largest taxing unit. Its
exercise of its constitutional power to tax is administered by the In-
ternal Revenue Service, and ostensibly is for the purpose of generating
sufficient revenues to conduct its activities.[237] Revenue collection is
described as the motivating purpose of the federal tax program, but
there are certainly important secondary effects on national and local
growth patterns. Several of these are briefly listed below.

(1) Fed by a national excise tax on gasoline and other automo-
tive products, the creation of the federal Highway Trust Fund,[238]
had undoubtedly determined the spatial characteristics of postwar
urban growth and energy consumption trends, not to mention its impact

on environmental quality. The federally aided highways built from the proceeds of the fund have set the framework for our automobile-centered suburban society. Continued growth based on this foundation is being actively opposed on many grounds.

(2) Next, the personal income tax deduction for single-family homeowner's mortgage interest payments has often been cited as a contributing factor in prompting the pervasive phenomenon of urban sprawl.[239] With the aid of this tax policy, postwar population growth has been funneled into suburban single-family residences.

(3) Federal corporate tax policy has acted in myriad ways to encourage industrial development. These actions have had an indirect yet highly powerful effect on land use decisions by influencing location patterns of residential and commercial growth.

(4) Other federal tax policies have also acted to spur development (for example, dependency deductions for large families, capital gains treatment for purchases and speculation in land, accelerated depreciation deductions for the construction of certain types of buildings). It is clear that the effect of these federal policies is considerable. In an uncoordinated and probably unintended way, these federal tax policies have influenced the form and the amount of growth and development in the postwar period. Unfortunately, these policies have not been guided by any problem-specific set of goals and objectives related to a notion of federal growth policy. If any thought was given to the developmental implications of these programs, it was probably assumed that growth is inherently good. In reality, many tax provisions were established by legislative amendments to the federal tax regulations at the insistence of various interest groups. The long-term land use implications of these changes were rarely considered.

Even if a comprehensive federal growth policy had been in existence, federal tax policy would probably not have become a primary developmental control technique because of its national scope, basic revenue collecting purpose, inherent inflexibility, and because it is limited by administrative rigidity. Further, federal taxes do not as directly involve the individual's holding and conversion of land as do local property taxes and preferential assessment plans; finally, local taxes are administered at a closer level to the taxpayer. For these reasons, we will in this section emphasize state, county, and municipal taxation mechanisms and policies.

## Local Tax Policy

The power of county and local units of government to impose a tax on the ownership of real property and improvements is derived from a statutory grant of authority from the state constitution.[240]

The exercise of the property tax has provided the main source of revenue for local governments throughout the nation, and has served to
finance most of their public services. However, because of its mode
of operation in many states, property taxation has been identified as
a primary cause of land conversion and development. Since land is
assessed at its ''highest and best'' use value and not as its actual land
use or productive value, owners of land used for agricultural, forest,
and other undeveloped purposes are often forced by the high tax level
to sell to a developer. In that way, development pressures acting
through the property tax cause land conversion and the sprawl phenomenon. Also, through mass subdivision, prime agricultural land at
the urban fringe is removed from cultivation.

In response to this phenomenon, a significant number of states,
including North Carolina, have instituted preferential tax assessment
measures to enable certain owners to retain agricultural, forest, or
other open land.[241] A recent study found that 34 states employed this
mechanism.[242] Preferential assessment policies have been difficult
to administer fairly. Some states allow assessment reduction solely
to agricultural land, and require yearly verification that the landowner
intends to maintain agricultural use. Others extend this tax benefit
to holders of forest and other open land. The intent of this type of
legislation appears to be to serve the interest of the small farmer
who cannot withstand spiraling property tax costs, and who truly
wishes to pursue his agricultural vocation. This has been a politically
attractive proposal in most states. However, it is not intended to act
as a corporate tax advantage, permitting land speculators to hold land
at low assessments before deciding to develop. To counteract this
danger of abuse, some of the states with agricultural tax exemption
or use valuation schemes have provided for tax penalties for those
who subsequently decide to subdivide. North Carolina, for example,
has enacted such a provision.[243] Under its plan, the difference between the present use value and the regular or highest and best use
value acts as a tax lien on the property, and is carried on the tax
records as deferred taxes. If the landowner disqualifies himself by
changing his land use, then the taxes deferred for the five years preceding become immediately due and payable with interest. The interest due on these deferred taxes is set on a sliding scale of two percent for the first month and three-fourths of a percent for each month
thereafter.[244] Furthermore, if the owner fails to list his change of
land use, he is subject to a ten percent penalty based on the total deferred taxes plus interest accrued.[245] California, under the Williamson Act, also taxes well-defined classes of agricultural land at a reduced rate in return for a landowner's obligation not to develop his
land for at least ten years.[246] This restrictive obligation is enforce-

able, and its breach by a landowner activates a stringent tax-deferral penalty charge of fifty percent.

The agricultural or undeveloped use tax mechanism appears to be the most common state-wide tax policy directed at growth issues. Its avowed intent is to preserve farm and other open land for many different reasons, the management of development being but one. Some have argued that the system does not discourage development, even if it uses tax penalties, since land speculators can use the deferred taxes to offset long-term capital gains realized by the sale of the land. Consequently, the speculator is benefited whether he develops or not. These criticisms must be acknowledged, and legislative means must be found to avoid such unintended results.

Also, the state-wide application of the technique diminishes its flexibility, since it is difficult to coordinate with local or county development planning. Unfortunately, tax measures are bound by legal uniformity restrictions limiting their use by local government. This is not to imply that preferential assessment policy cannot be used to manage growth, but it does emphasize the importance of using the technique as part of a systematic planning framework, and not as an independent tax policy. Thus, its application in a state effort to phase growth appears to be a more promising use. For instance, a section of the North Carolina Constitution could possibly serve as the basis for a tax policy approach to growth management strategies in that state. Section 2(4) of Article 5 provides for "special tax areas." The General Assembly is empowered to enact general laws authorizing local governmental bodies "to define territorial areas and to levy taxes within those areas, and in addition to those levied throughout the county, city or town, in order to finance, provide, or maintain services, facilities, and functions in addition to, or to a greater extent than those financed, provided or maintained for the entire county, city or town." This language could lay the groundwork for a tax structure guiding growth into areas where public services were already in existence or were provided for by a capital improvements plan. These higher, additional taxes would be levied on development in nonplanned areas.

Other state taxation mechanisms currently in use also influence development of land. State corporate income taxes, state real and personal property taxes, and tax classification procedures all can influence industrial location decisions, and often reflect an interstate rivalry for economic development. Some local units of government have the power to exempt desirable industrial land users from property taxes for specified periods of time. When this is done, the land use and environmental effects of attracting industry are subordinated to the economic interests of the area. Indeed, in many cases these policies have not been part of a state-wide or regional managed growth strategy, although their impact on growth is apparent.


Alternative Tax Policies


Tax Base Sharing

Tax base sharing has been another attempt to ameliorate the inadequacies of local property tax financing of more and higher quality public services. It has been suggested as a means to avoid competition for property tax revenues between neighboring taxing units, and to attain a more equitable balance of taxation levels among communities. By viewing the multi-county region or the state as an interdependent economic and developmental body with common interests and priorities, tax base sharing leads to more rational individual decisions affecting land use. This concept has been put into practice in the Minneapolis-St. Paul metropolitan area,[247] and has been proposed for the state of Maryland.[248] Katharine C. Lyall, the author of the tax base sharing proposal for Maryland, has stated that traditional local property taxation has resulted in a scramble for revenues in which one community is pitted against another. ''Such competition, driven by short run necessity, has produced widespread 'fiscal zoning,' the neglect of national long-run land use and public infrastructure planning, and the sacrifice of important environmental assets and open space to the more immediate needs of the competition for growth at any price.''[249]

Tax base sharing plans seek to capture a portion of the future increases in the commercial and industrial tax base, to tax them at a uniform rate, and then to distribute the resulting revenues according to a predetermined formula. This method establishes a ''growth pool'' that is collected and distributed every year. It need be noted that only future growth is shared by the larger unit, and that in both plans only a part of that increase is taken from the local taxing unit (40 percent in Minnesota and 60 percent in Maryland). Residential growth and all existing commercial and industrial land uses are taxed by the locality at whatever rate it chooses.

The tax base sharing system has been hailed as providing many benefits to local communities and to the state itself.[250] First, the competition among jurisdictions for revenue-producing industrial and commercial growth will ease. Second, the impetus to practice fiscal zoning will decrease due to equalized revenue distribution. Third, open space will be preserved and the environment enhanced, since there will no longer be a driving need to develop land to finance public services. Fourth, local autonomy will remain secure because the localities retain the authority to tax, relinquishing only a part of the tax base. Fifth, tax base sharing has a stabilizing effect by providing a more even flow of revenues to the community. "In rapid growth periods, when it can better afford it, a jurisdiction contributes more to the growth pool than in maturer periods when growth is slower. Since receipts depend upon population and average residential values, for a constant level of residential wealth a jurisdiction receives more [growth pool funds] in slow growth periods when it needs [them] most."[251]

Although the ramifications of such a program are not clear at this time and the political realities of regional cooperation make chances for adoption slight, tax base sharing must still be recognized as a potential tool for managing growth. Perhaps a modified regional tax base program could be manipulated to give additional tax revenues to jurisdictions where growth is desired under a regional plan. Other possibilities can be envisioned but since they all stem from the notion of regional financing and decision making, they remain politically unrealistic.

## The Development Tax

Another taxation mechanism which has been used to manage growth is the development tax.[252] Under this plan a developer must pay a fixed fee to the local government for the right to build within its jurisdiction. The fee, or development tax, would be uniform and related to the type and amount of construction. Ostensibly, there would be a relationship between the local impact of the development planned and the amount of the tax. Cost-benefit analysis could serve as the foundation for determining the level of the fees to be charged. In this way the tax could be viewed as a financial substitute for the conventional practice of subdivision land dedication or reservation. The funds yielded from the development fee could be allocated as development occurred to provide for the public services necessitated by the approved growth. This plan has the obvious deficiency of being temptingly exclusionary, depending upon its application by the local government. And it has no inherent relationship to any metropolitan or regional development plan. If many communities autonomously decide to impose development taxes at various unequal rates, fiscal zoning could be reinforced.

A review of the literature makes it apparent that public taxation policies have not been considered the most promising approach to the management of growth. The response to our questionnaire seems to verify this. In addition, several proposed tax policies face an uncertain reception in the courts, and some would invariably require statutory foundation and possibly constitutional amendment. Although taxation has been long recognized as an influential policy mechanism in other fields, other regulatory devices such as moratoria, timed development ordinances, and capital improvement planning are more widely used and thought to be more effective in phasing development.

As part of their study of managed growth, the authors prepared and administered a survey instrument which sought information regarding the prevalence of various growth control techniques and an evaluation of their effectiveness. The survey results are fully reported in Chapter 4 of this study. The survey was sent to 117 planning agencies throughout the nation that were believed to be concerned with growth management issues. Of these 117, 81 responded, a response rate of 69 percent. They were asked to specify whether their agency was utilizing any of the governmental and planning techniques listed in the questionnaire. They could respond by checking one of the following choices: (1) presently using the tool, (2) formerly used the tool, (3) intend to use the tool, (4) and have not used and do not intend to use the tool. "Preferential tax policies" was listed as one of the 22 techniques. Of the 75 respondents to this question, only 14 indicated that they presently were using them. One said that he had formerly used preferential tax policies, and only 13 indicated that they intended to use it in the future. The great majority, 47 (64 percent), expressed no interest in tax policy at the present or in the future. Of those stating that they are using this tool only three—Tulare County, California, San Luis Obispo, California, and Rochester, Minnesota—felt that it had been very effective as a growth management strategy. This lack of interest in taxation as a planning method stems partially from a belief held by planners that tax policy is beyond the realm of their competance, and, more importantly, beyond their influence. But most respondents who evaluated the tax policy found it generally to be ineffective whenever applied. This lack of confidence is probably justified by experience, since most tax policies have not been undergirded with a set of land use goals and objectives. Until this integration takes place, tax policy cannot be effectively used by planners and local governments.


## NOTES


1. See, e.g., the discussion on the delegation of these powers to localities in the section of this chapter on the adequate public facilities ordinance,

2. N.C. Gen. Stat. Sections 160A-381, 160A-383, 153A-339, 153A, 341.

3. Comment, "Large Lot Zoning," 78 Yale L.J. 1418 (1969) [hereinafter Large Lot Zoning].

4. 311 Mass. 560, 42 N.E. 2d 516. See also Schmandt, "Municipal Control of Urban Expansion," 39 Fordham L. Rev. 637 (1961) [hereinafter Schmandt].

5. Regional Plan Association, Spread City 13-14 (1962). Also see Note, "Exclusionary Zoning and Equal Protection," 84 Harv. L. Rev. 1645, note 30 (1971); Sussna, "Residential Densities: A Patchwork Placebo," 1 Ford. Urb. L.J. 127, 132 (1972).

6. Large Lot Zoning, supra note 3, at 1426.

7. Sussna, supra note 5, at 132.

8. See Becker, "The Police Power and Minimum Lot Size Zoning," 1969 Wash. U.L.Q. 263, 285-89.

9. Schmandt, supra note 4, at 653. See also Cutler, "Legal and Illegal Means for Controlling Urban Growth on the Urban Fringe," 1961 Wisc. L. Rev. 370.

10. "Very Low Density Zoning," Working Paper No. 3 for the Md.-Nat'l Capital Park and Planning Comm'n (1968).

11. Large lot zoning for this purpose has been accepted by the courts for some time. See, e.g., Bogert v. Township of Washington, 25 N.J. 57, 135 A.2d 1 (1957) where a one-acre minimum lot size was upheld in an area without public sewer facilities. See also Hagman, Urban Planning and Land Development Control Law 81 (1971).

12. See generally, Freilich, "Interim Development Controls: Essential Tools for Implementing Flexible Planning and Zoning," 49 J. Urb. L. 65 (1971).

13. For cases upholding large lot zoning on such grounds, see, e.g. Steel Hill Development, Inc. v. Town of Sanbornton, 469 F.2d 956 (1st Cir., 1972); Salamar Builders Corp. v. Tuttle, 29 N.Y.2d 221, 275 N.E. 2d 585 (1971).

14. See Coke and Liebaum, "Political Values and Population Density Control," 37 Land Economics, 347, 350 (1961). In a recent Supreme Court decision, Justice Douglas, writing for the majority, noted: "A quiet place where yards are wide, people few, and motor vehicles restricted are legitimate guidelines in a land-use project addressed to family needs. This goal is a permissible one. . . ." Village of Belle Terre v. Boras, 416 U.S. 1, 9 (1974).

15. Id., at 350-52. See also Note, "Snob Zoning—A Look at the Economics and Social Impact of Low Density Zoning," 15 Syracuse L. Rev. 507, 514-18, (1964) [hereinafter Snob Zoning]; Babcock and Bosselman, "Suburban Zoning and the Apartment Boom," III U. Penn L. Rev. 1040, 1062-65 (1963).

16. Buchanon v. Warley, 245 U.S. 60 (1970); Clinard v. City of Winston-Salem, 217 N.C. 119, 6 S.E.2d 867 (1940).

17. It has long been realized that localities can not directly set minimum housing costs. A commentator noted 25 years ago that "Provisions requiring that building erected on property cost a stipulated minimum amount, while common in restrictive covenants, have rarely been inserted in zoning ordinances. In the two reported cases where such zoning regulations were tested in the courts they were held unconstitutional." 50 Columbia L. Rev. 202, 204-5 (1950). See also, Note, "Snob Zoning: Must a Man's Home be a Castle?" 69 Mich. L. Rev. 339 (1970).

18. Snob Zoning, supra note 15, at 521.

19. Urban Land Institute, The Effects of Large Lot Size on Residential Development 9 (Tech. Bul. 32, 1958).

20. Id., at 10.

21. Large Lot Zoning, supra note 3, at 1419.

22. Sussna, supra note 5, at 132.

23. Id.; Urban Land Institute, supra note 19, at 8; Snob Zoning, supra note 15, at 514-18, 521.

24. See, e.g., Public Health Service, HEW, Environmental Health Planning Guide 45 (1967), for guidelines on the relationship between lot size and the feasibility of public sewerage.

25. See Large Lot Zoning, supra, at 14; National Comm'n on Urban Problems, Building the American City 213-15 (1968).

26. Mandelker, The Zoning Dilemma 42 (1971).

27. See, e.g. note 2 supra, and accompanying text. A 1961 survey of the case law on the subject concluded that lot sizes of one acre were seldom invalidated; Schmandt, supra note 4, at 639. All of those which have been invalidated seem to have been based on constitutional grounds, rather than on the authority granted in the enabling act.

28. See, e.g., Heaton v. City of Charlotte, 277 N.C. 506, 178 S.E.2d 352 (1971); Durham County v. Addison, 262 N.C. 280, 136 S.E.2d 600 (1964); Helms v. City of Charlotte, 255 N.C. 647, 122 S.E.2d 817 (1962).

29. However, where large lot zoning is being used to establish holding zones, a landowner may well be able to compel the issuance of a special use permit if the locality cannot adequately justify its holding zone to the courts. Hagman, supra note 11, at 120.

30. Becker, supra note 8, at 269.

31. U.S. Const. Amend. 5; U.S. Const. Amend 14, Section 1.

32. See Becker, supra note 8, at 304-07.

33. Id., at 306.

34. Hagman, supra note 11, at 92.

35. See, e.g., Nebbia v. New York, 291 U.S. 502 (1934); See also cases cited at note 29 supra; Large Lot Zoning, supra note 3, at 1435-37; But see, Appeal of the Township of Concord, 439 Pa. 466, 268 A.2d 765 (1970).

36. See, e.g., Appeal of Girsh, 437 Pa. 237, 263 A.3d 395 (1970); National Land and Investment Co. v. Easttown Township Bd. of Adjustment, 419 Pa. 504, 215 A.2d 597 (1965). Southern Burlington Co. NAACP v. Township of Mount Laurel, 67 N.J. 151, 336 A.2d 713, cert. denied U.S. (1975).

37. See generally Walsh, "Are Local Zoning Bodies Required by the Constitution to Consider Regional Needs?" 3 Conn. L. Rev. 244 (1971).

38. Shapiro v. Thompson, 394 U.S. 618, 634 (1970).

39. See, e.g., Large Lot Zoning, supra note 3, at 1437-41.

40. Id., at 1438-39. The Massachusetts Zoning Appeals Law, Mass. Gen. Laws Ann. ch. 40B, Sections 20-23 (Supp. 1973), is a variation of this proposal for administrative solution of the problems. Basically, it establishes a framework through which qualified applicants for subsidized homebuilding can bypass local regulations which prevent the construction of low-income housing. See, Note, "The Massachusetts Zoning Appeals Law: First Breach in the Exclusionary Wall," 54 Boston L. Rev. 37 (1974).

41. Note, "A Zoning Program for Phased Growth: Ramapo Township's Time Controls on Residential Development," 47 N.Y.U.L. Rev. 723, 723 (1972). [hereinafter Zoning Program for Phased Growth].

42. See generally Zoning Program for Phased Growth, supra note 41, at 723-24; Note, "Time Control, Sequential Zoning: The Ramapo Case," 25 Baylor L. Rev. 318, 326 (1973) [hereinafter Time Control, Sequential Zoning]; Comment, "Golden v. Town of Ramapo: Establishing a New Dimension in American Planning Law," 4 Urb. Law. ix (Summer, 1972) [hereinafter Establishing a New Dimension]; Franklin, "Controlling Urban Growth—But For Whom?" at 4 (1973).

43. Time Control, Sequential Zoning, supra note 42, at 326.

44. See Note, "Time Controls on Land Use: Prophylactic Law for Planners," 57 Cornell L. Rev. 82, 845-47 (1972) [hereinafter Time Controls on Land Use]; Kaiser, Elfers, Cohn, Reichert, Hufschmidt, and Stanland, Promoting Environmental Quality through Urban Planning and Control 153-54 (1973).

45. See, e.g., Green, Clark, May, and Fagin, "Clinic: Development Timing," Planning 1955 at 81; Cutler, "Legal and Illegal Methods for Controlling Community Growth on the Urban Fringe," 1961 Wis. L. Rev. 370; Schmandt, "Municipal Control of Urban Expansions," 29 Fordham L. Rev. 637 (1961); Fagin, "Regulating the Timing of Urban Development," 20 Law and Cont. Prob. 298 (1955).

46. Fagin, supra note 45, at 300-02.

47. Id., at 303-04.

48. Bosselman, "Can the Town of Ramapo Pass a Law to Bind the Rights of the Whole World?" 1 Fla. S.U.L. Rev. 234, 238 (1973).

49. Bureau of the Census, U.S. Dep't of Commerce, 1970 Census of Population, PC (1).

50. See Time Control, Sequential Zoning, supra note 42, at 327.

51. Ramapo Planning Board, Development Plan 20 (July, 1966). The studies leading to this plan were financed by a grant under section 701 of the Housing Act of 1964.

52. See Zoning Program for Phased Growth, supra note 41, at 727, n. 22.

53. Franklin, supra note 42, at 15. See also Bosselman, supra note 48, at 239.

54. Golden v. Planning Board of the Town of Ramapo, 30 N.Y.2d 359, 366-67, 285 N.E.2d 291, (1972).

55. Pertinent sections of this ordinance are reproduced in "Growth Controls," 24 Zoning Digest 99, at 68 (1972). See also Franklin, supra note 2, at 15-18. A quite similar ordinance has been proposed for Fairfax County, Virginia, and is reproduced in full in Appendix 1.

56. Amendments to the Town of Ramapo Building Zone Amended Ordinance of 1969, Section 46-13.1 (B) [hereinafter Zoning Ordinance].

57. Id., Section 46-13.1 (D).

58. Id., Section 46-13.1 (E) (1) (a).

59. Id., Section 46-13.1 (E) (1) (b).

60. Golden v. Planning Board, supra note 54. See Bosselman, supra note 48, at 240-42. These contentions are discussed at length below; see text accompanying notes 64-74.

61. 30 N.Y.2d 359, 285 N.E.2d 291 (1972).

62. "Establishing a New Dimension," supra note 42, at ix.

63. See, e.g., Franklin, supra note 42; Bosselman, supra note 48.

64. See, e.g., Schloss v. Jamison, 262 N.C. 108, 136 S.E.2d 691 (1964); Zopfi v. City of Wilmington, 273 N.C. 430, 160 S.E.2d 325 (1968); Heaton v. City of Charlotte, 277 N.C. 506, 178 S.E.2d 352 (1971); Keiger v. Winston-Salem Bd. of Adjustment, 281 N.C. 715, 190 S.E.2d 175 (1972).

65. Useful discussion of these issues with particular application to the Ramapo case may be found in Zoning Program for Phased Growth, supra note 1, at 732-39; Time Controls on Land Use, supra note 44, at 839-41.

66. Dep't of Commerce (1926 rev.). The Act is reprinted in full, 4 R. Anderson, American Law of Zoning 26.01 (1968).

67. The statute considered in the Ramapo decision was N.Y. Town Law § 261 (McKinney 1965).

68. The New York provision is N.Y. Town Law § 261 (McKinney 1965).

69. No. 525-1970, at 18 (Sup. Ct. Rockland County).

70. 37 App. Div. 2d 326, 244, 324 N.Y.S. 2d 178, 186.

71. 30 N.Y. 2d at 371, 285 N.E. 2d at 297.

72. 30 N.Y. 2d at 383, 285 N.E. 2d at 305.

73. 30 N.Y. 2d at 387, 285 N.E. 2d at 307.

74. See text accompanying note 68, supra.

75. See, e.g., Fasano v. Washington Co., 507 P.2d 23 (Ore. 1973) and Baker v. City of Milwaukee, 533 P.2d 772 (Ore. 1975). See generally Sullivan and Kessler, "Twenty Years After—Renewed Significance of the Comprehensive Plan Requirement," 9 Urban L. Ann. (1975); Tarlock, "Consistency with Adopted Land Use Plans as a Standard of Judicial Review: The case Against," 9 Urban L. Ann. (1975).

76. See discussion of "The Taking Issue" supra, Chapter 2.

77. See discussion of "Equal Protection of the Laws" supra, Chapter 2.

78. See discussion of "The Right to Travel," supra, Chapter 2.

79. See U.S. Const. Amend. 5; U.S. Const. Amend. 14, Section 1.

80. See, e.g. Williamson v. Lee Optical Co., 348 U.S. 483 (1955); West Coast Hotel v. Parrish, 300 U.S. 379 (1937); Nebbia v. New York, 291 U.S. 502 (1934).

81. This point was readily accepted in Golden v. Planning Bd. 30 N.Y. 2d at 376-78.

82. See section A of this chapter, supra, "Large Lot Zoning." See also Zoning Program for Phased Growth, supra note 41, at 744-49.

83. See National Land and Invest. Co. v. Easttown Twp. Bd. of Adjustment, 419 P. 504, 215 A.2d 597 (1965).

84. See Southern Burlington Co. NAACP v. Township of Mount Laurel, 67 N.J. 151, 336 A.2d 713, cert. denied ____ U.S. ____ (1975). Also see Franklin, supra note 42, at 20-22; Time Controls on Land Use, supra note 4, at 834.

85. See text accompanying note 64, supra.

86. For a full discussion of the taking issue, see supra, Chapter 2.

87. Some commentators have argued that the reduction of local property taxes during the period in which the land was restricted from being developed constituted compensation. However, this reduction merely reflected a change in the assessed value of the property, and, as property taxes are always levied only in relation to the assessed value, it was not in any sense compensation for the reduction in value itself. See Zoning Program for Phased Growth, supra note 41, at 167.

88. A discussion of the equal protection issue as applied to the Ramapo ordinance may be found in Zoning Program for Phased Growth, supra note 41, at 757-59.

89. See Franklin, supra note 42, at 22-23. Also see the discussion of the "two-tier test," supra in the section on "Equal protection of the laws in Chapter 2.

90. See generally Shapiro v. Thomson, 394 U.S. 618 (1969);
Edwards v. California, 314 U.S. 160 (1941).

91. See Elliot and Marcus, "From Euclid to Ramapo: New Directions in Land Development Controls," 1 Hofstra L. Rev. 56, 90 (1973).

92. See Franklin, supra note 42, at 32.

93. Bosselman, supra note 48, at 243.

94. Id.

95. Franklin, supra note 42, at 26.

96. Id.

97. Zoning Program for Phased Growth, supra note 41, at 729.

98. Franklin, supra note 42, at 18.

99. Mandelker, Speech before ALI-ABA Conference, Land Use and The Regulation of Development-II (Nov. 16, 1973).

100. Mandelker, The Zoning Dilemma 42 (1971). See also Bosselman, supra note 48, at 245-48.

101. See Franklin, supra note 42, at 29; Bosselman, supra note 48, at 251-52.

102. See, e.g., Franklin, supra note 42; Bosselman, supra note 48, at 248-50.

103. Bosselman, supra note 48, at 250.

104. Id., at 249-50.

105. Comment, "The Limits of Permissible Exclusion in Fiscal Zoning," 53 Boston U.L. Rev. 453, 456 (1973).

106. Franklin, supra note 42, at 27.

107. Bosselman, supra note 48, at 248. For a more detailed treatment of proposals for introducing regional planning perspectives in this respect, see Id., at 257-65.

108. Housing and Development Reporter, Vol. 1, no. 12, F-3 [hereinafter cited as HDR].

109. HDR, Vol. 2, no. 18, A-2 and A-3. See also, HDR, Vol. 2, no. 14, A-1.

110. In other states, similar action has been threatened. For example, North Carolina, the Department of Water and Air Resources has threatened to deny building permits in a portion of Raleigh if sewer capabilities are not improved. Similar proceedings are being undertaken in a number of other communities.

111. HDR, Vol. 1, no. 4, D-2.

112. HDR, Vol. 1, no. 6, F-2.

113. HDR, Vol. 1, no. 14, F-2.

114. HDR, Vol. 1, no. 4, D-1.

115. HDR, Vol. 1, no. 8, F-2.

116. HDR, Vol. 1, no. 4, D-3.

117. HDR, Vol. 1, no. 12, F-2.

118. HDR, Vol. 1, no. 4, D-1.

119. HDR, Vol. 1, no. 8, F-2.

120. HDR, Vol. 1, no. 14, F-2.

121. HDR, Vol. 2, no. 18, F-3.

122. Cited in "The Sewer Moratorium as a Technique of Growth Control and Environmental Protection," Rivkin/Carson, Inc., HUD Contract No. H-2095R, June, 1973, at 15-18.

123. Id., at 16, table 8.

124. Id., at 17, table 9.

125. Id., at 11-14.

126. Id., at 14, table 6.

127. Id.

128. Id., at 15.

129. 30 N.Y. 2d, 285 N.E.2d 291 (1972). See the discussion of the adequate public facilities ordinance supra, Chapter 2.

130. Id., at 14, table 7.

131. HDR, Vol. 1, no. 4, D-1.

132. HDR, Vol. 1, no. 2, D-1.

133. HDR, Vol. 1, no. 6, F-1.

134. HDR, Vol. 1, no. 14, F-1.

135. HDR, Vol. 1, no. 12, F-2.

136. HDR, Vol. 1, no. 4, D-3.

137. HDR, Vol. 1, no. 4, D-1.

138. HDR, Vol. 1, no. 4, D-1.

139. HDR, Vol. 1, no. 12, F-2.

140. HDR, Vol. 1, no. 14, F-2.

141. HDR, Vol. 1, no. 4, D-1.

142. HDR, Vol. 1, no. 4, D-1.

143. HDR, Vol. 1, no. 6, F-1.

144. HDR, Vol. 1, no. 8, F-1.

145. Id.

146. HDR, Vol. 1, no. 6, F-1. See also, HDR, Vol. 1, no. 14, F-1.

147. HDR, Vol. 1, no. 14, F-2.

148. HDR, Vol. 1, no. 18, F-1.

149. See the survey response from the Marin County Planning Department, on file at the Center for Urban and Regional Studies, Chapel Hill, N.C.

150. HDR, Vol. 1, no. 6, F-1.

151. HDR, Vol. 1, no. 7, C-3 and C-4.

152. HDR, Vol. 1, no. 6, F-1. See also HDR, Vol. 1, no. 8, F-1, and no. 12, F-1.

153. Personal interview, March 28, 1974.

154. "The Sewer Moratorium as a Technique of Growth Control and Environmental Protection," Rivkin/Carson Inc., HUD Contract No. H-2095R, June, 1973 at 3.

155. Id.

156. Id., at 18.

157. See the discussion of "The Right to Travel," supra, Chapter 2.

158. See Appendix 2.

159. D. Heeter, Toward a More Effective Land-Use Guidance System: A Summary and Analysis of Five Major Reports (Planning Advisory Service Report No. 250, 1969).

160. National Commission on Urban Problems (Douglas Commission), Building the American City 252-53 (1968).

161. President's Committee on Urban Housing (Kaiser Committee), A Decent Home 25-26 (1968). There is also a great deal of local interest in the use of land banking for growth management purposes. See, e.g., Livingston and Blayney, Santa Rosa Optimum Growth Study 108-12 (1973).

162. D. Shoup, Advanced Land Acquisition by Local Governments: Benefit-Cost Analysis as an Aid to Policy 16 (1968).

163. For a general discussion of the Montgomery County School Site Advanced Acquisition Program, see id., at 65-84.

164. Id., at 71.

165. Id., at 81.

166. Id., at 82.

167. For a general discussion of the Richmond program, see id., at 85-97.

168. Id., at 93.

169. Id., at 15.

170. C. Van Alystne, Land Bank Handbook; Advanced Acquisition of Sites for Low and Moderate Income Housing (1972).

171. Note, "Public Land Banking: A New Praxis for Urban Growth," 23 Case Western Reserve L. Rev. 897, 915-16 (1972) [hereinafter Public Land Banking].

172. E. Kaiser et al., supra note 44, at 365.

173. See Shoup, supra note 162, at 15.

174. Id., at 84.

175. See Public Land Banking, supra note 171, at 899.

176. Passow, "Land Reserves and Teamwork in Planning Stockholm," 36 J.A.I.P. 179 (1970).

177. K. Parsons, Canadian Land Banks (planning Advisory Service Report No. 284 (1972).

178. Id., at 10.

179. Clawson, "Urban Sprawl and Speculation in Suburban Land," 38 Land Economics 99 (1962).

180. Hamilton, "Public Land Banking Real or Illusory Benefits?" 13 (University of British Columbia Commerce, Jan. 1974).

181. S. Kamm, Land Banking: Public Policy Alternatives and Dilemmas 49 (1970).

182. See National Comm'n on Urban Problems, supra note 160, at 422.

183. See Parsons supra note 177, at 6.

184. S. Kamm, Reducing Land Costs Through Improvements in the Market Mechanism: A Potential System of Land Exchange Banks (1970).

185. See Kamm, supra note 181, at 13.

186. See Hamilton, supra note 180, at 17.

187. See Kamm, supra note 181, at 11.

188. See Public Land Banking, supra note 171, at 931.

189. Montgomery County Code §§ 26A-1 to 26A-4 (1965).

190. Wis. State § 80.64 (1973).

191. Mass. Const. § 11.

192. See Hamilton, supra note 180, at 18.

193. See Kamm, supra note 181, at 11-14.

194. See Public Land Banking, supra note 171, at 938.

195. Id., at 939.

196. Wisconsin Annotated Statutes § 62.22(1).

197. See, e.g., N.C. Const. art. 5 § 3.

198. See Public Land Banking, supra note 171, at 938.

199. See Kamm, supra note 181, at 41.

200. See Shoup, supra note 162, at 70.

201. See Kamm, supra note 181, at 30.

202. G. Edwards, Land, People and Policy 60 (1969).

203. See Passow, supra note 176, at 184.

204. P. R. Laws Ann. tit. 23 § 311M(f) (1964).

205. N.Y. Unconsol. Laws § 626316 (McKinney supp. 1971).

206. Carlor Co. v. City of Miami, 62 So.2d 897 (Fla. 1953), cert. denied 346 U.S. 821 (1953).

207. Vance County v. Royster, 271 N.C. 53, 60,155 S.E.2d 790, 796 (1967).

208. Chicago Land Clearance Commission v. White, 411 Ill. 310, 104 N.E.2d 236, cert. denied 344 U.S. 824 (1952).

209. 348 U.S. 26 (1954).

210. Redevelopment Agency of San Francisco v. Hayes, 122 Cal. App. 2d 777, 266 P.2d 105, cert. denied, 348 U.S. 897 (1954).

211. Commonwealth v. Russo, Opinion No. 67-172, El Tribunal Supremo de Puerto, Decembre 7, 1967, Appeal dismissed, 393 U.S. 14 (1968).

212. F. Bosselman, Alternatives to Urban Sprawl: Legal Guidelines For Government Action 49 (Research Report No. 15, National Commission on Urban Problems, 1968).

213. 57 Iowa Law Review 126 (1971).

214. A. Strong, Open Space for America 50 (1965).

215. Id.

216. D. Hagman, Public Acquisition and Disposal of Lands 12 (1970).

217. See Shoup, supra note 162.

218. U. Grundlach, Land Policies: Netherland 101-102 (U.N. Secretariat, Housing, Building and Planning, Bulletin No. 71953).

219. K. Parsons, Public Land Acquisition for New Communities and the Control of Urban Growth 20 (Center for Urban Development Research, Cornell University, 1973).

220. See Public Land Banking, supra note 171, at 909.

221. See Parsons, supra note 177, at 8.

222. U.S. Bureau of the Census, Statistical Abstract of the United States, 1969 190 (1969).

223. Public Land Law Review Commission, One Third of the Nation's Land (1970).

224. 43 U.S.C. §§ 461, 711-31.

225. 40 U.S.C. § 471.

226. Public Land Law Review Commission, One Third of the Nation's Land 57.

227. C. Stoddard, What's Ahead for Our Public Lands, 139-48.

228. See Public Land Law Review, supra note 223, at 82.

229. In the famous Veazie Bank case, 8 Wall. 533 (1869), which challenged the right of the State of Maryland to tax federal currency, Daniel Webster, arguing for the federal government, uttered the phrase, ''the power to tax is the power to destroy.'' Since that time, many attorneys have made similar claims, but usually on behalf of their clients against the federal government.

230. 195 U.S. 27 (1904).

231. 259 U.S. 20 (1922).

232. 345 U.S. 22 (1953).

233. 300 U.S. 506 (1937).

234. N.C. Const. Art. V, § 2 (2) (1973).

235. Id., at § 2 (1).

236. N.C. Gen. Stat. § 105-283 and 284.

237. Title 26, United States Code (1970).

238. Section 209 of the Act of June 29, 1956, ch. 462, Title II, 70 Stat. 397.

239. 26 U.S.C. § 163 and 164 (a) (1) (1970).

240. See N.C. Gen. Stat. ch. 105, art. 16 and 22.

241. N.C. Gen. Stat. 105-277.2-277.7 (1973). The statute is reproduced in full in Appendix 4.

242. International Association of Assessing Officers, ''Use-Value Farmland Assessments,'' in Environmental Comments 3, no. 21 (May 1975).

243. N.C. Gen. Stat. 105-277.4 (c) (1973).

244. N.C. Gen. Stat. 105-360 (a) (3) (1973).

245. N.C. Gen. Stat. 105-277.5 (1973).

246. F. Parker, Land Policy Alternatives for North Carolina 136-37 (1972). For tax penalty provisions, see also, Section 426 of the California Revenue and Taxation Code.

247. Minnesota Laws 1971—Extra Session, Chapter 24, S.F. No. 10, pp. 2286-99.

248. K. Lyall, "Tax Base Sharing: A Partial Solution to Some Problems of the Local Property Tax" (Center for Metro. Planning and Resources, The Johns Hopkins University, 1973).

249. Id., at 1.

250. Id., at 6-7.

251. Id., at 7.

252. Housing and Development Reporter, Vol. 2, No. 12, F-2. In addition, the charging of fees for development expenses incurred by the local government unit is not uncommon.

## FURTHER REFERENCES ON TAXATION POLICY

Cooke and Power, "Preferential Assessment of Agricultural Land," 47 Florida Bar J. 636 (1973).

Delogu, "Taxing Power as Land Use Control Device," 45 Denver L. J. 279 (1968).

Gaffney, "Land Planning and the Property Tax," 35 J.A.I.P. 178 (1969).

Gurko, "Federal Income Tax and Urban Sprawl," 48 Denver L. J. 329 (1972).

K. Lyall, Tax Base-Sharing: A Partial Solution to Some Problems of the Local Property Tax (The Johns Hopkins University Center for Metropolitan Planning and Research, 1973).

Note, "Site Value Taxation: Economic Incentives and Land Use Planning," 9 Harv. J. Legis. 115 (1971).

Note, "Toward Optimal Use of Land, Property Tax Policy and Land Use Planning," 55 Calif. L. Rev. 856 (1967).

Pickford and Shannon, "Harnessing Property Taxes and Land Use Planning," 38 Planning 304 (1972).

Property Taxation, Housing and Urban Growth (Urban Institute Symposium, 1970).

Stocker, "Taxing Farmland in the Urban Fringe," 45 J. Farm Econ. 1131 (1963).

Sullivan, "Greening of the Taxpayer: The Relationship of Farm Zone Taxation in Oregon to Land Use," 9 Willamette L. J. 1 (1973).

Walker, "Some Observations on Land Value Taxation," 38 Tax Policy, June-July, 1971, at 6.

Williams, "The Three Systems of Land Use Control," 25 Rutgers L. Rev. 80 (1970).

# 4

## SURVEY OF
## SELECTED COMMUNITIES

In addition to examining reports of various development timing efforts in the planning and legal literature, an evaluation of governmental attempts to manage growth through the timing of development should reflect the experience gained by communities that have actually implemented such programs.

In order to obtain an impression as to how the various development timing techniques have performed, communities that had undertaken development timing efforts were surveyed.[1] It should be emphasized that this was not a random sample of planning offices. The report being made is an evaluative one—its purpose is to discover what tools and techniques are being used in communities to time development and, more importantly, how the planning directors in these communities feel the devices have worked; how effective they have been and what problems have been involved with their use. Therefore, the survey was specifically aimed at and sent to those agencies with active experience in the growth management field—those on the cutting edge of the development timing effort. The results of the survey should not be read as representing the experience of all planning agencies in the United States. These results are offered rather as a report of the experiences of a number of planning agencies that have attempted to time development.

The survey was mailed in the early part of February 1974, to 117 selected planning agencies across the United States.[2] There was broad geographical representation, with some emphasis naturally on those areas of the country that have experienced the most severe growth pressures and were thereby the first to establish growth management programs with development timing components. Local, metropolitan, county, and regional agencies of varying sizes and levels of sophistication were surveyed. By the cutoff date, April 30, 1974, 81 replies had been received, a 69 percent response rate. Of these, 77 responses contained usable questionnaires.

## PROBLEM PERCEPTION

As is indicated by Table 2, the overwhelming majority of the agencies consulted perceived development timing to be one of their agencies' most important problems. This has not always been the case. When asked how important this problem was in the 1960s, a majority (59 percent) responded that it was either "relatively unimportant" or "important but not critical." When estimating its importance in the future, however, only 18 percent of the respondents thought the problem would have such a low priority. And it should be noted that most of these evaluations of future relative unimportance came from localities which are already for the most part fully developed, and which cannot expand geographically.

Nearly three-fourths (73 percent) of the respondents indicated that, at the present time, development timing problems are crucial ones for their agencies. They rated development timing as either their "most critical" one or as a "very important" one. Eighty-two percent of the agencies consulted believe the problem will assume this high level of importance by the 1980s. Therefore, attempts to control the timing of urban development will in many instances be one of the major efforts of these planning agencies in the coming years.

## TABLE 2

### Importance of Development Timing Problems
### in the Agency's Jurisdiction
### (in percentage)

|                             | Distribution of Responses | | |
| --------------------------- | ----- | ------- | ----- |
| Perceived Importance        | 1960s | Present | 1980s |
| Our most critical problem   | 10    | 26      | 21    |
| A very important problem     | 31    | 47      | 61    |
| Important, but not critical | 32    | 22      | 12    |
| Relatively unimportant      | 27    | 4       | 6     |
| N =                         | (62)  | (68)    | (66)  |

Source: Data compiled by the authors.

## USE OF TIMING DEVICES

The respondents' use of various regulations, controls, and incentives for control of the timing of development in their jurisdictions is summarized in Table 3. The tools and techniques are listed in order, the widely used being listed first.

Not surprisingly, the traditional zoning ordinances and subdivision regulations are the most frequently used tools. Only three techniques are currently in use by a majority of the respondents to time development—subdivision regulations, agricultural zoning, and large lot zoning (more than two acres). Also, as anticipated, the less frequently used timing devices include both those which are new and relatively untested, such as the adequate public facilities ordinance and the concept of transferable development rights, as well as those which are thought to require large capital outlays for effective start up and operation such as impact zoning and land banking. However, because of the high perceived importance of the development timing problem, a significant number of the agencies surveyed intend to use these newer and more expensive tools in the future. This was particularly true with the adequate public facilities ordinance, which 19 percent of the respondents indicated an intent to use. Furthermore, this 19 percent "intend to use" rating, which was the highest given to any single timing device, is probably unrealistically low due to the lack of a common, widely used term for the concept. A number of agencies commented in the open-ended section of the questionnaire that they intended to adopt "Ramapo-style" ordinances or "adequate public facilities" ordinances, but failed to check "intend to use" for the "timed development" ordinance. These specific responses alone would push the "intend to use" figure to almost 25 percent.

## PERCEIVED EFFECTIVENESS

Evaluation of the effectiveness of these techniques for the timing of development is a difficult task. The establishment of strict criteria for review, collection of data, and complex modeling needed for an objective evaluation of their performance was beyond the scope of this project. However, taken by themselves, subjective academic predictions of their potential impact are clearly unsatisfactory. So, in an effort to get an impression of the relative effectiveness of a number of devices which may be used to time development, the survey questioned the planning directors about how the various devices have worked in their jurisdictions.

TABLE 3

Use of Tools and Techniques for Development Timing
in Order of Frequency of Use

(N = 77)

| Type of Tool or Technique | Percent of Respondents | | | |
| --- | --- | --- | --- | --- |
| | In Use | Formerly Used | Intend To Use | Not Used or No Response |
| Subdivision regulations | 81 | — | 3 | 16 |
| Agricultural zoning | 57 | 3 | 6 | 34 |
| Large lot zoning (2+acres) | 52 | 1 | 3 | 44 |
| Water/Sewer extension moratoria | 42 | 3 | 6 | 49 |
| Down zoning | 40 | 4 | 12 | 44 |
| Performance standards | 39 | — | 13 | 48 |
| Public investment policies | 34 | — | 16 | 50 |
| Zoning change moratoria (legislative) | 34 | 6 | 1 | 59 |
| Building permit moratoria | 34 | 9 | 1 | 56 |
| Water/Sewer hookup moratoria | 32 | — | 4 | 64 |
| Urban service areas | 30 | — | 16 | 54 |
| Development districts | 25 | — | 10 | 65 |
| Public land management | 21 | — | 9 | 70 |
| Subdivision moratoria | 19 | 3 | 3 | 75 |
| Preferential tax policies | 18 | 1 | 17 | 64 |
| Adequate public facilities ordinance (timed development) | 13 | — | 19 | 68 |
| Zoning change moratoria (administrative) | 12 | — | — | 88 |
| Transfer of development rights | 10 | — | 14 | 76 |
| Impact zoning | 9 | — | 14 | 77 |
| Land banking | 6 | — | 10 | 84 |
| Other acquisition policies | 5 | — | 1 | 94 |
| Others | 18 | — | 2 | 80 |

Source: Data compiled by the authors.

The survey results indicate that the effective use of any particular device depends to a great extent on local circumstances—the strength and type of localized developmental pressures, the design of the particular device, and the way in which it is administered. As is shown in Table 4, many individual devices that were ranked as ''very effective'' in some jurisdictions, were often rated ''not effective'' in others. Therefore, the experiences of these communities indicate that no technique can be recommended as the single solution to development timing problems. Rather, the responses generally indicate that a mix of devices will need to be selected by each community. The appropriate mix will then have to be carefully designed and administered so as to address the particular needs and development timing problems of each area attempting to manage its growth.

Even with the above reservations, some initial grouping of tools and techniques according to their perceived effectiveness is desirable. In Table 4, all devices which received ten or more evaluations are grouped according to their relative perceived effectiveness. This grouping is accomplished through the use of an effectiveness index. The index score is the average effectiveness rating given to the technique by evaluating agencies.[3] Those devices receiving fewer than ten evaluations are not grouped with the others because of the high variance in the index score that can result from a single agency's experience with the device, given the small number of evaluations being averaged. Therefore, the survey results on the effectiveness ratings of these devices are reported under ''others.''

The devices which the planning directors consulted rated as having the highest relative effectiveness in controlling the timing of development are generally those that approach the problem most directly. The three devices rated as having the highest effectiveness are all moratoria that have immediate, direct, and highly visible impacts on the rate of development. In fact, these three—moratoria on water/sewer hookups, subdivision approvals, and water/sewer extensions—were the only three techniques which a majority of the respondents rated as being ''very effective'' in the control of the timing of development. A fourth moratorium device, the building permit moratorium, received the next highest number of ''very effective'' ratings—47 percent. However, it received a lower average rating because in many communities a large number of building permits were outstanding at the time the moratorium was imposed. This backlog of permits allowed development to continue unabated for some time after the moratorium had been imposed, thus lessening its immediate impact and perceived effectiveness.

An examination of the six devices in the ''most effective'' category indicates that one of the newer tools, the adequate public facilities ordinance, may have a high level of perceived effectiveness in the

## TABLE 4

Perceived Effectiveness of Development Timing Tools and Techniques

| Type of Tool or Technique [no. of agencies with experience making evaluation] | Effectiveness Index* | Percent of Respondents Having Experience With the Tool and Rating it as: | | | |
|---|---|---|---|---|---|
| | | Very Effective | Moderately Effective | Slightly Effective | Not Effective |
| **More Effective** | | | | | |
| Water/Sewer hookup moratoria (23) | 1.35 | 65 | 35 | — | — |
| Subdivision moratoria (17) | 1.59 | 53 | 35 | 12 | — |
| Water/Sewer extension moratoria (31) | 1.61 | 55 | 35 | 3 | 6 |
| Public investment policies (24) | 1.71 | 42 | 46 | 13 | — |
| Urban service areas (22) | 1.77 | 36 | 50 | 14 | — |
| Building permit moratoria (32) | 1.78 | 47 | 34 | 13 | 6 |
| **Less Effective** | | | | | |
| Subdivision regulations (57) | 1.95 | 33 | 44 | 18 | 5 |
| Zoning change moratoria (legislative) (28) | 1.96 | 39 | 29 | 29 | 4 |
| Performance standards (29) | 1.97 | 34 | 38 | 24 | 3 |
| **Least Effective** | | | | | |
| Down zoning (31) | 2.16 | 32 | 32 | 23 | 13 |
| Development districts (17) | 2.18 | 29 | 35 | 24 | 12 |

| | | | | | |
|---|---|---|---|---|---|
| Agricultural zoning (43) | 2.19 | 28 | 40 | 19 | 14 |
| Public land management (16) | 2.25 | 19 | 38 | 44 | — |
| Large lot zoning (2+ acres) (39) | 2.31 | 23 | 38 | 23 | 15 |
| Preferential tax policies (14) | 2.50 | 14 | 29 | 50 | 7 |
| Others (fewer than 10 evaluations) | | | | | |
| Zoning change moratoria (administrative) (9) | 2.44 | 22 | 33 | 22 | 22 |
| Timed development (or adequate public facilities) ordinance (8) | 1.88 | 38 | 38 | 25 | — |
| Transfer of development rights (7) | 2.43 | 14 | 43 | 29 | 14 |
| Impact zoning (7) | 1.86 | 29 | 57 | 14 | — |
| Land banking (4) | 2.25 | 50 | — | 25 | 25 |
| Other acquisition policies (4) | 1.50 | 50 | 50 | — | — |

*Effectiveness index: This rating is the mean effectiveness rating given to the tool or technique by the evaluating agencies. It is derived by assigning a score of 1 for a rating of very effective, 2 for moderately effective, 3 for slightly effective, and 4 for not effective. The index is the average (mean) score. Thus, the lower the index number, the higher the perceived effectiveness.

<u>Source:</u> Data compiled by the authors.

future, as it combines elements of these six devices into a single technique. The adequate public facilities ordinance places a moratorium on future development until sufficient public facilities, including water and sewer capabilities, are in place. When tied to a capital improvement plan which stages expansion in a rational manner, public investment policies can be directly related to development moratoria, and the tools can be used together to manage growth.[4]

Several of the tools that are most widely used were rated among the least effective devices for controlling the timing of development. For example, agricultural zoning and large lot zoning are often the first techniques used by localities in their attempts to time development, primarily because already existing zoning ordinances could be amended easily. However, as Table 4 indicates, these "back door" attempts to time development were rarely characterized as "very effective." In fact, 38 percent of the respondents indicated that large lot zoning was either "not effective" or only "slightly effective" in controlling the timing of development. This evaluation from practicing planners adds credence to the discussion in preceding chapters criticizing these tools for their many adverse secondary effects.

## REPORTED OBJECTIVES

In addition to examining what techniques have been used and how effective the planning directors feel they have been, further insight can be gained into the development timing experience of these communities by a closer examination of the objectives which development timing strategies are designed to accomplish. As Table 5 indicates, most strategies are directed toward a number of objectives, many of them overlapping, most of them complementary, but a few of them conflicting.

The objectives, as reported by the planning directors, readily refute the proposition that most efforts to time development are part of a "no-growth" movement. Of all of the objectives subscribed to by those respondents attempting to time development, the desire to limit population growth was among those with the fewest adherents. Of the 77 respondents, only 11 (14 percent) indicated that the limitation of population growth was one of their objectives. Furthermore, most of these 11 were from communities which are already rather densely populated.

According to the survey, the objective most widely ascribed to is a desire to limit development until the necessary services for it can be provided. Eighty-four percent of the respondents noted that

TABLE 5

Objectives of Development Timing Strategies

(N = 77)

| Objective | Percentage of Agencies Identifying it as One of Their Objectives |
|---|---|
| Provision of adequate urban services | 84 |
| Reduction of urban sprawl | 78 |
| Environmental protection | 78 |
| Preservation of open space | 66 |
| Preservation of character of community | 60 |
| Environmental enhancement | 58 |
| Preservation of local amenities | 55 |
| Reduction of traffic congestion | 53 |
| Improvement of governmental financial stability | 44 |
| Prevention of overcrowding of schools | 38 |
| Control of rate of population growth | 30 |
| Reduction of speculation in private land market | 26 |
| Protection of property values | 19 |
| Control of housing costs | 17 |
| Limitation of population growth | 14 |
| Lowering of tax rates | 10 |
| Others | 12 |

Source: Data compiled by the authors.

their development timing strategies were aimed at assuring the provision of adequate urban services. Related objectives, such as reduction of urban sprawl, were also ranked highly. This reflects a commitment to the management of growth, not to stopping it.

Still, several objectives that may imply an eventual ultimate ceiling on growth were frequently mentioned. Environmental protection, preservation of open space, local amenities, and community character, and environmental enhancement were all checked as valid objectives by a majority of respondents. However, in most communities the planning directors felt these objectives could still be served through programs of planned growth. An end of growth was felt to be by no means necessary in most instances. Even so, environmental

objectives could be furthered only by severe restriction of growth in
certain areas, and the responding planners often recommended a regional approach to growth management through development timing
in order to balance all interests involved.


## GENERAL RESPONSES


In addition to eliciting statistical information, the questionnaire
asked respondents to describe a number of aspects of their experience
with development timing. The following summary seeks to convey the
general tone of the responses.

When queried as to why the techniques they had rated as not being effective did not work well, several general lines of response
emerged. The reason most frequently cited for their ineffectiveness
was a lack of adequate commitment to development timing concepts
by local governing boards faced with strong developmental pressures.
When confronted with pressure from developers, the planners surveyed
thought the decision makers all too often either changed their policies
or granted individual variances to particular development projects.

Another problem that was mentioned almost as frequently was
the lack of a coordinated regional approach to the problems of development timing. Governmental fragmentation, with its resultant intergovernmental competition and general lack of coordination, was seen
to be a major block to effective growth management.

Three other problems were also identified, though less frequently, by the planning directors as important factors in the lack
of success of efforts to time development. First, the lack of clear
authority from the state to use the techniques the directors perceived
to be necessary for effective growth management was cited. Most local governments are still operating within a framework of state enabling legislation that is closely modeled after the Standard State
Planning and Zoning Acts prepared forty years ago. Many of the directors felt that this framework is inadequate for modern problems
of timing development. A second factor noted by the respondents was
a general lack of understanding of the techniques for development
timing, on the part of both planners and governing bodies. They felt
that in many instances the devices were being adopted with little understanding of their secondary and long-term impacts. A final point
mentioned was the lack of any overall systems approach to development timing efforts. Elements of this problem include the lack of
clear, explicit timing goals and objectives and the uncoordinated use
of a wide range not only of planning tools and techniques, but of all
current governmental activities.[5]

When asked what changes were necessary for more effective timing of development in their jurisdictions, the planning directors' suggestions for reform closely parallel the problems identified above.

The change most frequently mentioned was the need for an improved legal framework within which development timing efforts would be undertaken. The directors generally stressed the need for a clearer statement in state legislation of the nature and extent of mechanisms available for local developmental control. They often coupled this need with an expressed desire for explicit permission to use new and more powerful tools as components of their development timing strategies.

A second reform, also widely suggested as necessary for effective development timing control, is the more frequent use of a regional approach to development timing problems. The directors acknowledged that development timing problems largely transcend political boundaries and jurisdictions, and that as a result coordinated intergovernmental and regional approaches are necessary. There were few concrete suggestions as to how this regional input should be obtained, but there was widespread agreement that it was necessary. In a later question which queried the directors as to the extent of present state and regional coordination of development timing efforts, the overwhelming majority reported that very little if any coordination was currently being practiced.[6] The few that had established some workable system of regional cooperation in development control were very enthusiastic about the results.

A third frequently suggested change in the governmental approach to growth management through development timing was a call for increased use of coordinated growth guidance systems. The respondents felt that when development control techniques were not being applied in a coordinated fashion towards a single set of objectives, the techniques often conflicted. In fact, in many cases they even counteracted each other. Somewhat related to this was the need expressed for greater predictive modeling capabilities. That is, the directors felt a real need for information about what the impacts of the various timing devices would be before they were actually imposed.

Finally, there was a feeling among a number of the respondents that in addition to building the technical competence of governments to deal with problems of development timing, successful growth management will require increased awareness of the problems involved and commitment to their solution by both elected officials and the public at large. They felt that, without this widespread political support for the concept of development timing, any strategies developed by planners would have a low probability of success.

This need was amplified by the responses to another survey question—one which inquired into the existence of strong political reaction resulting from agency attempts to time development. In those jurisdictions with relatively successful development timing efforts, the typical response was that there was strong and widespread public support for the concept of staging growth. Opposition by developers and large landowners was also common in those areas and tended to moderate the thrust of timing efforts. However, widespread political support for growth management prevented these pressures from subverting governmental timing efforts. In other communities, where there was no widespread support for development timing among the citizens, the short-term financial interests of those favoring continued uncontrolled growth (generally identified as some developers and large landowners) prevented any effective timing of development.

A final question in the open-ended section of the questionnaire asked whether there had been any litigation resulting from local attempts to time development. Since this survey was directed primarily toward those planning agencies with active development timing programs, it might be expected that a large number of them would be involved in litigation on this subject. This was not the case. The overwhelming majority reported that no litigation on their development timing efforts had been initiated. Several expected such litigation in the future, but at the present time, only 9 of the 77 responding agencies could report any direct litigation on the development timing issue. Of these challenges to governmental efforts to regulate the timing of development, three cases were settled before trial, two are still pending at the initial trial court level, and four have been decided at the trial court level. None of these latter four cases has yet been appealed to higher courts.[7]

The results of these reported judicial decisions are inconclusive for several reasons. First, only trial court decisions that might be changed on appeal are involved. Secondly, different timing techniques were used in each community. Finally, local design and administration even of the same tool will vary considerably with each application; this will have important impacts on the outcome of judicial challenges. Because of these factors, no firm conclusions can be drawn from these cases regarding the ultimate legality of development timing strategies.

## NOTES

1. The survey instrument, which was mailed to planning directors in selected communities, is reproduced below in Appendix E.

2. The sample itself was devised by using a combination of the following: a literature search (including a wide range of professional planning and legal publications, newspapers, and lay periodicals); a study of conference reports and materials; and, results of previous surveys undertaken by study participants. While the more widely publicized timing efforts were of course surfaced through the literature and conference materials, the previous survey results (which were obtained through a nationwide random sample of planning agencies of all sizes) uncovered a number of lesser-known efforts.

3. See the footnote to Table 4 for the precise method of ascertaining index scores.

4. For a complete analysis of the adequate public facilities ordinance, see Chapter 3.

5. See the section on large lot zoning, Chapter 3.

6. The only exception to this total lack of state and regional coordination seems to be in the area of provision of water and sewer facilities and control of related health problems.

7. Of course, one well known case, Golden v. Planning Bd. of the Township of Ramapo, 30 N.Y.2d 359 (1972), has been decided by a state's highest court. Though this case is not covered in the survey report, a full discussion of that Court's upholding of a development timing strategy may be found in the section on the adequate public facilities ordinance, in Chapter 3. The four cases which have been decided at the trial level include challenges to the development timing efforts in three California communities—San Jose, Petaluma, and Livermore—and in Loudoun County, Virginia. Only in San Jose was the initial decision favorable to the local government. However, on appeal to the Ninth Circuit Court of Appeals, the governmental effort in Petaluma was upheld, F.2d (1975). Other ongoing litigation of note involves development timing efforts in Boulder, Colorado and Fairfax County, Virginia.

# 5

The judicial system has come to be an important factor in planners' decisions in recent years. The constitutional issues involved in techniques to time development and manage growth form a common thread through this book. How to satisfy the court? How to choose tools that will avoid litigation? How to prepare a defense in the process of planning in anticipation of judicial challenge? These questions, even if they most often are not explicitly expressed, color a planner's choice of, or reluctance to use tools to manage growth. Planners have long recognized the political limitations on their work. Now it seems that the judicial system has made further inroads into their ability to pursue goals, choose tools, and use technical expertise for the future good of the community they serve.

It would not be surprising if some planners viewed this new development in planning with dismay, even despair. In a number of decisions, handed down in both federal and state courts all over the country, the courts have set a tone that planners can no longer ignore. Developers, civil rights groups, and others affected by growth management efforts will undoubtedly continue to turn to the courts in cases of conflict.

Planners most commonly come to court on the defense. This is not a comfortable position. Quite understandably, a planner would prefer to spend his time implementing the policy he conceived, developed, and got approved, rather than justifying its use in court. In preparing his growth management program, since he knows something of the legal concept of judicial precedent, he may attempt to review court decisions on similar cases, only to find no apparent pattern. Taken overall, the courts' decisions may seem to be without fundamental rules, even capricious. In one community a moratorium is declared invalid. In another case, with what appear to be similar facts, the use of the tool is upheld. Even the process of finding out what decisions

have been made is difficult, because this is an active area of the law
in which new cases are constantly developing and decisions constantly
being overturned by higher courts. All levels of the judiciary are
hearing cases of this type. One can have only sympathy for the planner
facing this complex issue in his already complex world.

Given this new element in the planning area, is the planner
merely going to be moved further along the road of spurts and set-
backs, with little hope of having long-range effects on a community—
preserving what is good and unique in it, developing its assets, and
stemming the encroachment of undesirable changes? The planner's
task has always been complex. In school, at professional conferences,
and in the literature, he is exposed to concepts with great potential
for changing a community. He soon begins to appreciate the political
and social nature of his community, and learns how these concepts he
respects must be compromised to fit into it. At times these political
and social factors can seem to render any innovative planning impossible. Now the courts are presenting the planners with another battle-
ground. One cannot expect planners to welcome the courts' participation in the planning process.

However, there is another way of looking at this. In several recent cases the New Jersey Supreme Court has said that a growth
management program must take regional factors into consideration—
as principle planners have been espousing for years. The highest court
in the state of New York seemed to indicate that it would have struck
down the Ramapo program had it not taken into consideration in the
preparation of its plan the welfare of an area larger than its own jurisdiction. A federal district court held that the attempt of Petaluma,
California to limit growth was an infringement on the constitutional
right to travel because the policy interfered with normal movement
within the housing market in the region. Perhaps the courts' insistence that local growth management efforts be placed within a regional
context will lend support to planners who have been frequently frustrated by politicians with a purely parochial view.

In a similar way some courts are reinforcing the concept that
land use controls must be drawn in accordance with a comprehensive
plan. The Oregon Supreme Court recently held invalid a zoning ordinance that had not been brought into conformance with such a plan,
because the plan had been adopted subsequent to the zoning ordinance.
Cases from other states have drawn upon doctrines of administrative
law in reviewing variance and rezoning procedures. A logical extension of these cases would be to conclude that a comprehensive plan
is the legislative policy against which implementation of administrative action, such as zoning and subdivision control, is evaluated.

The Virginia Supreme Court, when Fairfax County refused to
change its zoning to a more dense residential use, ordered the county

to do so because such use had been anticipated in its adopted plan. The county argued that even though the plan did in fact anticipate such a use the time was not right for it because adequate public facilities were not available and that to change the zoning at this point would permit development in violation of state law. The county, however, was not able to point to any local policy indicating when, if ever, such facilities would be available. In contrast, in the Ramapo case, where the court found that the locality had committed itself to a capital improvements program which was an integral part of a comprehensive plan, the court permitted the locality to delay development for as long as 18 years. Thus the courts seem to be lending support to another fundamental concept of good planning: the comprehensive plan.

In addition, these cases indicate the danger of trying to do too much with too little. Urban development has many dimensions of which time is only one. Techniques of growth management must be carefully selected to deal with the specific objective to be affected. Where a number of dimensions are affected, the techniques must be orchestrated so that they complement each other, thus avoiding unwanted and unexpected effects.

A superficial reading of the early sections of this book may lead to despair for those who are attempting to manage urban growth. It is our conclusion, however, that the tools and techniques described in this book, and other growth management techniques as well, are likely to withstand challenge in the courts—but only if they are used with great skill and care.

ADEQUATE PUBLIC FACILITIES ORDINANCE
PROPOSED FOR FAIRFAX COUNTY, VIRGINIA*

9-701 General Considerations

The County of Fairfax, being a major urbanized area of the
Washington, D.C. metropolitan region, has been experiencing continuing unprecedented and rapid growth with respect to population, housing, economy, land development and utilization of resources, for the
past decade. Transportation, water, sewerage, schools, parks and
recreation, drainage, and other public facilities and requirements
have been and are being constructed to meet the needs of the County's
growing population, but the County has been unable to provide these
services and facilities at a pace which will keep abreast of the ever-
growing need. The rapid growth and spread of urban development is
creating encroachment upon and elimination of the open areas and
spaces of the County and loss of agricultural, horticultural and forest
uses which must be preserved in the public interest. The rapid growth
and urban sprawl is creating a series of major problems, including:
imbalance of growth between uses; inability to provide public services
to match private development; soaring tax rates due to inefficient provision of services; land speculation, environmental degradation of
natural landscape, flood plains, hillsides and stream valleys, uncontrolled character of private development; an inability to plan or implement planning, lack of time to develop solutions or adequate administrative and legal mechanisms and a lack of proper housing for
low and moderate income families needed to attract industrial and
commercial employment, for senior citizens and young families and
to meet the economic and tax needs of the County and serious problems of shortages of gasoline, heating fuel and energy by reason of
extended distances of urban sprawl for commutation, police, fire,
school and essential services and other public and private needs.

Faced with the physical, social, fiscal and environmental problems caused by the rapid and unprecedented growth, the County of

---

*This proposal is very similar to the ordinance adopted by the
Town of Ramapo, except that this ordinance provides bonus points for
the inclusion of low- and moderate-income housing.

Fairfax is adopting a new comprehensive plan to guide its future development and is adopting an official map and a capital outlay program
and plan so as to provide for the maximum orderly, adequate, and economical development of its future residential, industrial, commercial,
and public land uses and facilities including transportation, water,
sewerage, schools, housing, parks and recreation sites, open space,
drainage, preservation of agricultural, horticultural and forest uses,
flood plains, wetlands and environmental critical areas, and other
public facilities.

In order to insure that these comprehensive and coordinated
plans are not frustrated by disorganized, unplanned and uncoordinated
development which would create an undue burden and hardship on the
ability of the community to translate these plans into reality, the following objectives are established as policy determinations of zoning
and planning for the County of Fairfax:

1.   To economize on the capital and operating costs of public
facilities and services by carefully phasing residential development
so as to be consonant with adequate and efficient provision of public
improvements;

2.   To establish and maintain county control over the character,
direction, and timing of development;

3.   To establish and maintain a desirable degree of balance
among the various uses of the land;

4.   To establish and maintain essential quality of community
services and facilities;

5.   To preserve and protect open space land, and agricultural,
and forest uses;

6.   To preserve and protect the environment and environmentally critical areas;

7.   To preserve gasoline, heating fuel, and energy for vital public and private functions, wasted by useless urban sprawl and extended
roads, utilities, and development.

The County through its comprehensive plan, official map, capital outlay program and plan, zoning and subdivision regulations, open
space land commission laws, and complementary planning programs,
studies, ordinances and regulations has mandated a program of continuing improvements which is designed to ensure complete availability of all public facilities and services for all land within the urbanized area of the County and the urbanizing area of the County
within the next twenty (20) years, in accord with proper planning.
Haphazard, sprawling and uncoordinated development of land without
the adequate provision of public services and facilities will destroy
the continuing implementation and adoption of the program. Residential

development will be carefully phased so as to insure that all developable land will be accorded a present vested right to develop at such
time as services and facilities are available. Residential land which
has the necessary available minicipal facilities and services will be
granted approval. Residential land which lacks the available facilities and services will be granted approval for development at such
time as the facilities and services are indicated to be available by
the ongoing capital outlay program and plan of the County, or in which
the residential developer agrees to furnish such facility or improvement in advance of the scheduled program for improvement of the public sector.

These regulations are adopted pursuant to the authority of the
Constitution of the State of Virginia; the Planning, Subdivision of Land
and Zoning Law, Va. Code 15.1-427 to 15.1-503.2; the Urban County
Forms of Government Law, Va. Code 15.1-722 to 15.1-791; the Open
Space Land Act, Va. Code 10-151 to 10-158; the Special Assessments
for Agricultural, Horticultural, Forest or Open Space Real Estate Act,
Va. Code 58-769.4 to 58-769.16; by providing for comprehensive planning and zoning for the government, protection, order, conduct, safety,
health and well being of the persons and property in the County and
consistent with the purposes of expediting the provision of adequate
police and fire protection, transportation, water, sewerage, flood
protection, schools, parks, playgrounds, recreational facilities and
other public requirements; to preserve open space, agricultural, horticultural and forest uses; to assist in shaping the character, direction and timing of community development; and that the growth of the
community be consonant with the efficient and economical use of public funds.

## 9-702 Special Permit — Residential Development Use — Effective Date

Prior to the issuance of any building permit, special permit of
the Board of Supervisors, preliminary subdivision approval, final development plan or final site plan approval, for residential development
use, a residential developer or development agent shall be required to
obtain a special permit from the Board of Supervisors pursuant to
9-700 et seq.

The provisions of this section shall not be applicable to lots
contained in subdivisions preliminarily approved prior to the effective
date of this section.

This section shall become effective upon the date of adoption
of each section sheet (or sheets), properly identified and dated, and
constituting the "Official Zoning Map, Fairfax County, Virginia" as
provided in Article 2, Section 2-202 of this Ordinance, for each planning district of the County.

9-703 Procedure for Special Permit

1. The residential developer or residential development agent shall be required to submit an application to the Zoning Administrator in such detail and in such number of copies as shall be set forth in forms to be prepared by the Zoning Administrator, including a map showing the location of all land holdings of the applicant in the same development use. The zoning administrator shall review the application with respect to all standards set forth in Section 9-704 as to the availability of municipal services and facilities and projected improvements scheduled in the capital outlay program and capital outlay plan of the County. The Zoning Administrator may request reports from appropriate county, municipal, regional, state or federal agencies, boards of officials as may be required. Within forty-five (45) days of the submission of the application, the Zoning Administrator shall report his findings in writing with reason therefore to the Board of Supervisors, and the said Board shall proceed to notice the application for public hearing at the first regular meeting of the Board of Supervisors, not less than two weeks after the submission of the Zoning Administrator's written report.
2. The Board of Supervisors shall within thirty (30) days after conclusion of the public hearing render its decision in writing stating whether the application is approved or denied, and if approved, the Board of Supervisors shall render its determination as to the number of residential dwellings that shall be permitted to be built, and the year in which such development shall be permitted to proceed in accordance with the capital outlay program and plan.

9-704 Standards for the Issuance of Special Permits

No special permit shall be issued by the Board of Supervisors unless the residential development has available twenty-two (22) development points on the following scale of values:

(1) Sewers
　　　　(a) Public sewers available                        5 points
　　　　(b) Package sewer plants                           3 points
　　　　(c) County approved septic system In R-C district  3 points
　　　　(d) All others                                     0 points
(2) Drainage
　　　　Percentage of Required Drainage Capacity Available
　　　　(a) 100% or more                                   5 points
　　　　(b) 90% - 99%                                      4 points
　　　　(c) 80% - 89.9%                                    3 points

(d) 65% - 79.9%                                           2 points
(e) 50% - 64.9%                                           1 point
(f) less than 50%                                         0 points
(3) Improved Park or Recreational Facility Including Public School
                    Recreational Site
    (a) Within 1/4 mile                                   5 points
    (b) Within 1/2 mile                                   3 points
    (c) Within 1 mile                                     1 point
    (d) Further than 1 mile                               0 points
(4) State, County, or Town, Major, Secondary or Collector Road(s)
            Improved with Curbs and Sidewalks
    (a) Direct Access                                     5 points
    (b) Within 1/2 mile                                   3 points
    (c) Within 1 mile                                     1 point
    (d) Further than 1 mile                               0 points
(5) Fire House
    (a) Within 1 mile                                     3 points
    (b) Within 2 miles                                    1 point
    (c) Further than 2 miles                              0 points
(6) Police Station
    (a) Within 2 miles                                    3 points
    (b) Within 4 miles                                    1 point
    (c) Further than 4 miles                              0 points
(7) Elementary School (with sufficient capacity to absorb the number
    of children expected to inhabit the development without resorting
    to double sessions or other methods to handle overcrowding)
    (a) Within 1 mile                                     5 points
    (b) Within 1 1/2 mile                                 4 points
    (c) Within 2 miles                                    3 points
    (d) Within 2 1/2 miles                                2 points
    (e) Within 3 miles                                    1 point
    (f) More than 3 miles                                 0 points

All distances shall be computed from the proposed location of each
separate lot or plot capable of being improved with a residential
dwelling and not from the boundaries of the entire parcel, to the
boundaries of the public facility. The Board of Supervisors shall issue the special permit specifying the number of dwelling units that
meet the standards set forth herein.


Bonus for Low and Moderate Income Housing

Any residential developer who provides low and moderate income
housing units in his development shall receive the following bonus toward the twenty-two points required to obtain a special permit:

| (a) | 30% of total units | 4 points |
|-----|--------------------|----------|
| (b) | 25% of total units | 3 points |
| (c) | 20% of total units | 2 points |
| (d) | 10% of total units | 1 point |
| (e) | Less than 10% of total units | 0 points |

9-705  Vested Approval and Relief
   1.  Vested Approval of Special Permit

      A.   The Board of Supervisors shall issue an approval of
the application for special permit vesting a present right for the residential developer to proceed with residential development use of the
land for such year as the proposed development meets the required
points as indicated in the scheduled completion dates of the capital
outlay program and plan as amended.  If the residential development
fails to meet the required points for any period within the twenty (20)
year period of the capital outlay program and plan, the application for
special permit shall be denied.  Any improvement schedule in the
capital outlay program and plan more than one year from date of
application shall be credited as though in existence as of the date of
the scheduled completion.  Any improvement scheduled in the capital
outlay program or plan for completion within one year from the date
of application for the special permit shall be credited as though in
existence on the date of application.

      B.   A developer may advance the date of authorization
by agreeing to provide such improvements as will bring the development within the required number of points for earlier or immediate
development.  Such agreement shall be secured by either a cash deposit or surety bond sufficient to cover the cost of proposed improvement, the form, sufficiency, and amount of which bond shall be determined by the Board of Supervisors.  In application of this section the
developer shall be entitled to pay his pro-rata share of such off-site
improvements for reasonable sewerage and drainage facilities, in
accordance with regulations to be established by the Board of Supervisors, pursuant to Va. Code 15.1-466(i).

      C.   All approved special permits vesting a present right
to future development shall be fully assignable without restriction.

      D.   Nothing herein contained shall prevent such land from
being immediately used for all other purposes other than residential
development use, as is authorized by the zoning ordinance.

    2.  Relief

      Any residential developer or development agent who has
applied for a special permit from the Board of Supervisors pursuant

to this section, shall be entitled as of right, to apply within one year from the Board of Supervisor's determination granting the vested approval, or denial, to the Open Space Land Commission Ordinance, pursuant to Chapter 17A of the Fairfax County Code for:

A. A property owner holding less than five (5) acres an assessment benefit pursuant to 17A-9 Fairfax County Code (Va. Code 10-155) upon the property owner convening to the County a development easement or other interest in the property for the period of the restriction; or

B. A property owner holding five (5) or more acres, or agricultural, horticultural or forest lands taxation on the basis of a use assessment pursuant to 17A-10 Fairfax County Code (Va. Code 58-769.8)

The assessment shall reflect the extent to which the temporary restriction on residential development use of the land shall affect the assessed valuation placed on such land for purposes of real estate taxation and such assessed valuation on such land shall be reduced as provided above and pursuant to the Open Space Land Commission Ordinance as compensation for the temporary restriction placed on the land.

## 9-706 Variances

1. The Board of Supervisors shall have the power to vary or modify the application of any provision of 9-700 of this ordinance upon its determination in its legislative discretion, that such variance or modification is consistent with comprehensive planning for proper land use including the comprehensive plan, official map, capital budget and capital outlay program and plan upon which this ordinance is based and with the health, safety and general welfare of the County and its inhabitants.

2. Upon receiving any application for such variance or modification, such application shall be referred to the Planning Commission of Fairfax County for a report and recommendation of said Planning Commission with respect to the effect of the proposed variance or modification upon the comprehensive planning of the County including the comprehensive plan, official map, capital outlay program and plan, existing laws and regulations and the health, safety and general welfare of the County and its inhabitants.

3. All applications for a variance or a modification shall be filed with the Zoning Administrator who shall forward same within

two weeks to the Planning Commission for its report. Such report shall be made in writing and shall be returned by the Planning Commission to the Zoning Administrator within 30 days of such reference. The said Zoning Administrator shall forward said report to the Board of Supervisors, and the Board of Supervisors shall proceed to notice the application for public hearing at the first regular meeting of the Board of Supervisors not less than thirty (30) days after submission of the written report by the Planning Commission. The Board of Supervisors shall render its determination within thirty (30) days after the conclusion of the public hearing.

FAIRFAX COUNTY, VIRGINIA,
INTERIM DEVELOPMENT ORDINANCE

BE IT ORDAINED BY THE BOARD OF SUPERVISORS
OF FAIRFAX COUNTY:

Amend Chapter 30, by adding a new Article XIX, Interim Development Ordinance, said Article to read as follows:

Sec. 30-19.1   This Article shall be in full force and effect from the date of its enactment until June 30, 1975, the date established for the adoption of the complete official zoning map of the entire County. This Article shall apply to real property zoned under the Zoning Ordinance of 1959 as amended and revised.

Sec. 30-19.2   During the period while this Article is in full force and effect for all real property in Fairfax County:

(A)   No application shall be accepted for, nor any approval granted for, a special permit, a site plan or a preliminary subdivision plat which is tendered to the County after January 7, 1974, except as provided in Section (C) or (E) of this Article.

(B)   Nothing contained in this Article shall be deemed:
   (1) to preclude the County from consideration of any application for a special permit, a site plan or a preliminary subdivision plat which was submitted on or before January 7, 1974; or
   (2) to preclude the County from consideration of:
      (a) a renewal of a special use permit, a site plan, or a subdivision plat which was legally valid on or after January 7, 1973.
      (b) an amendment to
         (i) a valid site plan or special use permit, which involves only alteration or additions to existing buildings or uses when such addition does not exceed two thousand square feet or one-third of existing area, whichever is greater.

     (ii) a valid subdivision plat submitted and
approved under Chapter 23 or development
plan submitted and approved under Article XV
of this Chapter or under the RPC provisions of
Section 30-2.2.2 of this Chapter, where the
proposed amendment is consistent with the
prior approval.

(3) to abrogate or annul any prior approval lawfully
issued and in effect on January 7, 1974.

(C)

(1) Any applicant for, or holder, or his agents or
assigns, of:

     (a) a special permit;

     (b) a site plan;

     (c) a preliminary subdivision plat;

     (d) a development plan submitted under Article XV
of this Chapter;

     (e) a development plan submitted under the RPC
(Residential Planned Community) provisions of
Section 30-2.2.2 of this Chapter,

which special permit, site plan, preliminary subdivision
plat, or development plan has been approved or is
subsequently approved, may take whatever steps are
necessary, including application for such future
approval as is necessary to allow him to begin
construction on, or use of, the subject property.

(2) The Board of Zoning Appeals or the Board of
Supervisors may accept and consider application for
special use permits filed subsequent to January 7,
1974, where the applicant establishes that the
proposed use:

     (a) is a change of use within the same use
group which involves only alteration or additions
to existing buildings or uses when such addition
does not exceed two thousand square feet or
one-third of existing area, whichever is greater; or

     (b) is consistent with a general designation
which has been included on a plat or plan
submitted and approved under Chapter 23, under
Article XV of this Chapter, or under the RPC
provisions of Section 30.2.2.2 of this Chapter; or

     (c) is a tax exempt use as defined in Virginia
Code § 58-12.

(D)   No application for an amendment to the Zoning Ordinance of 1959 as amended and revised on the date of adoption of this Article shall be accepted or considered by the County during the period while this Article is in effect.

This provision shall not preclude the Board on its own motion, from consideration or adoption of an amendment to the zoning map, where:

(1) A court of competent jurisdiction has determined that the existing classification on any particular parcel or tract of land is improper; or

(2) An applicant for an amendment barred by this section has complied with the procedural requirements of the Board, and on the Board's request has postponed the hearing of such application to the harm or detriment of such applicant, his agent, or assigns.

(E)   No proposal for a public facility shall be subject to the provisions of this Article. A public facility shall include any facility identified as such under Virginia Code § 15.1-456 and any other facility financed directly in whole or in part by federal, state, or local government.

## PUERTO RICO LAND ADMINISTRATION ACT

Chapter 23
§ 311a.  Definitions

The following terms, whenever used in this chapter, shall have the following meanings, except where the context otherwise clearly indicates:

(a) "Administration" means the Puerto Rico Land Administration.

(b) "Board" means the Governing Board of the Administration.

(c) "Bonds" means bonds, notes, or other obligations or evidences of indebtedness.

(d) "Agency" means branch, department, bureau, commission, board, office, dependency, instrumentality, public corporation, political subdivision, or any other government body.

(e) "United States" includes the Federal Government and its agencies, territories, possessions and political subdivisions, and the states of the Union and agencies thereof.

§ 311b.  Puerto Rico Land Administration, creation; Governing Board, composition, term, compensation

(a) There is hereby created a body corporate and politic which shall constitute a public corporation or government instrumentality having a juridicial personality separate and apart from that of the Commonwealth of Puerto Rico, and shall be known as the Puerto Rico Land Administration.

(b) The powers of the Administration shall be exercised, and its general policy determined, by a Governing Board composed of the Governor of Puerto Rico, who shall be chairman, the Chairman of the Puerto Rico Planning Board, who shall be vice-chairman, the Secretaries of the Treasury, Public Works, and Agriculture, the Director of the Urban Renewal and Housing Corporation, the Economic Development Administrator, and two additional members to be appointed by the Governor, with the advice and consent of the Senate, for a term of four years and until their successors are appointed and qualify.

The members of the Board shall receive no compensation for their services as such.

## § 311c.  Executive Director

The Executive Director of the Administration shall be appointed by the Board, shall hold office at the will of the appointing authority and until his successor is appointed and qualifies, and shall discharge such duties and bear such responsibilities as may be assigned to him by the appointing authority, pursuant to the bylaws of the Administration. The bylaws of the Administration may provide for the delegation to the Executive Director of such powers and duties of the Administration as the Board may deem proper.

## § 311d.  Secretary

The Administration shall have a secretary, who shall be appointed by the Board. The Secretary shall hold office at the will of the appointing authority and until his successor is appointed and qualifies.

## § 311e.  Debts, contracts, finances, printed matter and property

The debts, obligations, contracts, bonds, notes, debentures, receipts, expenditures, accounts, funds, printed matter, and property of the Administration shall be deemed to be those of the said Administration and not those of the Commonwealth of Puerto Rico or of any agency, official or employee thereof.

## § 311f.  Duties and powers

The Administration shall have a juridical personality of its own and may exercise such rights and powers as may be necessary or proper for the carrying out of the purposes hereof, including, but not limited to, the following:

(a) To have perpetual succession;

(b) To approve, amend or repeal bylaws;

(c) To appoint all its officials, agents and employees, and to grant and impose on them such powers, faculties, responsibilities, and authority as it may deem proper; to determine their duties; to fix, change and pay such compensation as it may determine, subject to the policy, bylaws, regulations and procedures approved by the Board. All personnel matters of the Administration shall be regulated without subjection to the laws governing the Office of Personnel of the Government of Puerto Rico or to the rules and regulations promulgated by said Office;

(d) To adopt, alter, and use a seal which shall be judically noticed;

(e) To draft, adopt, amend, and repeal rules and regulations governing the policies of its activities in general, and to exercise and discharge the powers and duties granted to and imposed on it by law. Upon the approval and promulgation of said rules and regulations by the Board, the same shall have the force of law as soon as filed in Spanish and English in the offices of the Secretary of State. Such rules and regulations shall be published in the Bulletin (Register) of the Commonwealth of Puerto Rico and shall not later than ten days after filed in the office of the Secretary of State, be published in a newspaper of general circulation;

(f) To sue and be sued;

(g) To establish the accounting system required for an adequate control of all expenditures and revenues pertaining to or administered by it, in consultation with the Secretary of the Treasury;

(h) To have full powers for the carrying out of the public policy of the Commonwealth of Puerto Rico as herein established;

(i) To make contracts and to execute all instruments necessary or expedient in the exercise of any or all of its powers;

(j) To acquire property in any lawful manner, including, but without limitation, the following: by purchase, option of purchase, purchase by installments, at public auction, by lease, legacy, devise, assignment, exchange, gift, or by the exercise of the right of eminent domain in the manner provided by this act and the laws of Puerto Rico; and to hold, maintain, use and avail itself of, or utilize any real or personal property, including, but not limited to, securities and other movables or any interest therein, deemed by it necessary or desirable to carry out its purposes;

(k) To sell, grant options of sale, sell by instalments, convey exchange, lease or otherwise dispose of its property in the course of its normal operations, except by gift, which may only be made for the benefit of the Commonwealth of Puerto Rico and its agencies. There shall not be considered as a gift any disposal of property, or of any right or interest therein, which, in fulfillment of the purposes hereof may be effected by the Administration at a lower price than it paid for same, or lower than the value of such property, or right or interest therein, in the market;

(l) To sell or otherwise dispose of any real or personal property which in the judgment of the Administration is no longer necessary to carry out the purposes of this chapter, subject to the same limitation imposed thereupon by the preceding paragraph;

(m) To borrow money, give security and issue bonds for any of its corporate purposes or for the purpose of funding, refunding, paying, or discharging any of its outstanding or assumed bonds or obliga-

tions, and to secure payment of its bonds and of any and all other obligations by pledging, mortgaging, or otherwise encumbering all or
any of its contracts, revenues, income or property;

(n) To accept in its own behalf, or in behalf of the Commonwealth of Puerto Rico, financial aid of any nature, including subsidies,
gifts, advances and suchlike, from the Commonwealth of Puerto Rico
or its agencies, from the United States Government or its agencies,
and from private persons; to enter into contracts, leases, agreements,
or other transactions with both or any of such governments or their
agencies, and to expend the proceeds of the funds so received for the
purposes of this chapter;

(o) To have complete control and supervision of any and all of
its property and activities, including the power to determine the character of and necessity for all its expenditures and the manner in which
they shall be allowed, incurred, and paid, without regard to the provisions of any laws governing the expenditure of public funds, and
such determination shall be final and conclusive upon all officers and
employees of the Commonwealth of Puerto Rico, without prejudice to
the provisions of section 311i of this title;

(p) To prescribe by regulation the policies governing all matters with relation to the personnel of the Administration. Such policies shall, insofar as compatible with the efficient effectuation of the
purposes of the Administration, be similar to those governing the personnel of the commonwealth government;

(q) To acquire, in the manner provided in this chapter, private
property and keep it in reserve, for the benefit of the people of Puerto
Rico, for the use of the Commonwealth of Puerto Rico or its agencies.
Whenever properties or property rights are condemned for specific
purposes of public-work development and social welfare, such purposes shall be carried out within a period of years which shall never
exceed fifteen, from the date of acquisition. The property so acquired
may be assigned or conveyed to the Commonwealth of Puerto Rico or
its agencies, under reasonable terms and conditions;

(r) To enter, after obtaining permission to do so from the owner
or holder, or his representative, any land or premises, for the purpose of making surveys, taking measurements, or conducting investi-
gations with regard to the nature, conditions and price of such lands
or premises, for the purposes of this chapter. Should the owner or
holder, or his representative, refuse to grant permission to enter the
property for the above-mentioned purposes, any judge of the Court of
First Instance shall, upon presentation to him of an affidavit setting
forth the intention of the Administration to enter such lands or premises for the stated purposes, issue an order authorizing any official
or officials, or employee or employees of the Administration to enter
the property described in the affidavit, for the purposes mentioned in
this provision;

(s) To acquire real property, urban or rural, which may be kept in reserve towards facilitating the continuation of the development of public work and social and economic welfare programs which may be under way or which may be undertaken by the Administration itself, by the Commonwealth of Puerto Rico or its agencies, and by private persons for the benefit of the above-mentioned public entities or of the community, including, but not limited to, housing and industrial development programs, in order to prevent the inflation brought about by speculative practices in the purchase-sale of real estate and to allow for populational growth in an organized and planned manner;

(t) To promote and share in the fitting out of new areas anywhere in Puerto Rico, within the frame of the policies which will insure a better balance with regard to the needs of future communities, aiming, among other things, to preserve the natural values of the lands, beaches, forests, and landscapes; to insure the best conditions of health, safety, comfort, recreational facilities, essential services, and esthetic activities; to preserve historical values, to insure the utilization of lands on the basis of the most reasonable costs in behalf of the welfare of the community; to this end, but not to be construed as a limitation, to develop programs for the acquisition of the necessary lands, and for encouraging all kinds of projects, such as will favor such development, either on its own or through or jointly with agencies of the Commonwealth of Puerto Rico or of the Government of the United States, or with private entities;

(u) To barter for the purpose of improving the utilization of the lands;

(v) To exercise all necessary powers and rights for developing land rehabilitation projects through drying, draining, filling, irrigating, or any other proper means for increasing land utilization;

(w) To carry out by itself, or through or jointly with agencies of the Commonwealth or of the Government of the United States, or by means of covenants with private persons or entities, programs and works, including housing projects, to insure the most effective development and the fullest utilization, in keeping with the purposes of this chapter, of lands owned by the Administration, or by the Commonwealth or any of its agencies;

(x) To acquire any right or interest or easement in any property in order to: promote the development, utilization and maintenance of open areas in their natural state so as to protect bodies of water; to protect the public from the effects of floods; to preserve soils and forests; to preserve the beauty of places devoted to public use, including green areas and public parks; and to facilitate the use and development of areas which are in reserve for projects of public interest, especially those related to the health, safety and welfare of the inhabitants;

(y) To enter into agreements with the Commonwealth and its agencies so as to acquire real property for them; to sell real property owned by them, or intervene in or carry out the development of programs in connection with such property, subject to the laws that fix the official activities of said agencies. To such ends, the parties to these covenants are hereby authorized to make such transfers of funds as may be necessary;

(z) To establish, in disposing of any real property, all such conditions and limitations regarding its use or utilization as it may deem necessary and desirable to insure the fulfillment of the purposes of this chapter, so that the use made of said property will not facilitate or tend to create undesirable conditions, or conditions adverse to the public interest, which this chapter aims to protect. Whenever the Administration sells or otherwise disposes of property for the acquirer to erect thereon housing developments or any other type of project involving a subsequent sale to private persons, it may fix such restrictions as it may deem necessary for the effectuation of the purposes of this chapter. In any event, it shall include one limiting, through a proper formula, the profits to be had by the acquirer with respect to the land and all other costs of the project;

(a-1) To transmit, in perpetuity or for a limited time, to urbanizers, for housing developments, and to other persons for the undertaking of any work having social interest, any right, real or personal, or any interest in the lands that it may hold; and

(b-1) To sell, whenever it may deem it necessary and desirable, lands or any interest therein, at such price as it may consider reasonable in order to lower the cost of the houses or to fulfill any of the purposes of this chapter.

## § 311g.   Subdivision of lands

The Administration may, subject to the applicable regulations of the Planning Board, subdivide the lands acquired by any of the means authorized by law, according to the topography of the land, its fertility, the local conditions, and the desirable policies to achieve the best development or utilization of such lands for the benefit of the Puerto Rican community, and thus to fulfill the purposes of this chapter. The size and value of such lands shall be determined by the Administration on the basis of the existing needs in the zone, urban or rural, where a program or public work or activity is to be undertaken for the better utilization of such lands. The Administration shall promulgate the necessary regulations to fulfill the purposes of this section.

## § 311h.  Deposit and disbursement of funds

All funds of the Administration, including the proceeds from the sale of its bonds, shall be deposited with recognized depositories for funds of the Commonwealth of Puerto Rico, but such funds shall be kept in a separate account or accounts registered in the name of the Administration. Disbursements shall be made by the Administration according to its own regulations and budgets.

## § 311i.  Examination of accounts and books by Controller; report

The Controller of the Commonwealth of Puerto Rico shall, whenever he may deem it necessary, but at least once each year, examine all accounts and books of the Administration, and shall report thereon to the Legislative Assembly, the Governor, and any other public officer, as he may see fit. No provision of this chapter shall be construed as a limitation to the powers of the Controller of Puerto Rico.

## § 311j.  Conveyance of property and land to Administration

The public corporations of the Commonwealth are hereby authorized to assign and convey to the Administration, at the latter's request and under such reasonable terms and conditions as they may agree upon, without the need for auction or other legal formalities additional to the execution of the proper instrument, any property or interest therein, including property already devoted to public use, such as the Administration may deem it necessary or desirable to possess for the effectuation of its own purposes.

The Secretary of Public Works may, free of any cost whatsoever, convey to the Administration, with the approval of the Governor, such lands of the Commonwealth of Puerto Rico as said Administration may need for the effectuation of its purposes. This provision shall not be construed in the sense of authorizing the assignment or conveyance of property specifically devoted to other purposes by legislative provision.

## § 311k.  Property—Purchase and condemnation

On request of the Administration, the Commonwealth of Puerto Rico may acquire, by purchase, condemnation, or by any other lawful means, for the use and benefit of the Administration, in the manner provided for by this chapter and by the Commonwealth laws on condemnation, the title to any real property and the interests therein that may be necessary or convenient for its purposes. The Administration shall advance the necessary funds estimated as the value of the property or rights to be acquired. Any difference in value which may be decreed by the competent court may be paid from the public treasury, but the Administration shall be under obligation to reimburse said difference. After reimbursement in full is made, the title to said property shall be transferred to the Administration, upon order of the court to that effect. In those cases where the Governor of the Commonwealth of Puerto Rico should deem it necessary and convenient that the title to the property and rights so acquired be directly recorded in behalf of the Administration so as to speed up the fulfillment of the ends and purposes for which the same was created, he may so request from the court at any time within the condemnation proceedings, and the court shall so order. The power hereby conferred on the Governor shall not limit or restrain the authority of the Administration to institute itself the condemnation proceedings when it may deem it convenient.

## § 3111.  Declaration of public utility

All real and personal property or interests therein necessary to carry out the purposes of this chapter, are declared of public utility, also every work or project carried out by the Administration, and said real and personal property or any less estate or interest therein, may be condemned without the previous declaration of public utility provided in the General Law of Eminent Domain, sections 2901-2913 of Title 32, either by condemnation proceedings instituted by the Commonwealth of Puerto Rico, or directly by the Administration.

## § 311m.  Procedure for acquisition, disposal

(a) In any proceedings which have been or may be instituted by and in the name of the Administration for the acquisition of land for the purposes specified in this chapter, the Administration may file in the same cause, at the time the petition is filed or at any time before judgment is rendered, a declaration of taking for the acquisition and material delivery of the property the object of condemnation, signed by the person or entity empowered by law to seek the condemnation in question, declaring that said property is sought for the use of the Administration. Said declaration of taking and material delivery shall contain and be accompanied by: (1) a statement of the authority under which, and the public use for which, the acquisition of said property is sought; (2) a description of the property sufficient for the

identification thereof; (3) a statement of the estate or interest in said
property the acquisition of which is sought for the utilization purposes
specified in this chapter; (4) a plan, in the case of property which can
be so represented; (5) the fixing of the sum of money estimated by the
Administration to be just compensation for the property the acquisition
of which is sought.

(b) As soon as said declaration of taking and delivery is filed
and the deposit is made in the court, for the benefit and use of the
natural or artificial person or persons entitled thereto, of the amount
estimated as compensation and specified in said declaration, title to
the said property in fee simple absolute, or such less estate or interest therein as is specified in said declaration, shall vest in the Administration or in the Commonwealth of Puerto Rico, as the case may be,
and such property shall be deemed to be condemned and acquired for
the use of the Administration or of the Commonwealth of Puerto Rico.
The right to just compensation for the property shall vest in the person or persons entitled thereto; and said compensation shall be as-
certained and awarded in said proceeding and established by judgment
therein; and the said judgment shall include, as part of the just compensation awarded, interest at the rate of six per centum (6%) per
annum on the amount finally awarded as the value of the property as
of the date of taking, from said date to the date of payment; interest
shall not be allowed on so much thereof as shall have been deposited
and paid into the court. No sum so deposited and paid into the court
shall be subject to any charge for any reason whatsoever.

(c) Upon application of the parties in interest, the court may
order that the money deposited in the court, or any part thereof, be
paid forthwith for or on account of the just compensation to be awarded
in said proceeding. If the compensation finally awarded in respect to
said property, or any part thereof, shall exceed the amount of the
money so received by any entitled person, the court shall enter judgment against the Administration or the Commonwealth of Puerto Rico,
as the case may be, for the amount of the difference.

(d) Upon the filing of the declaration of taking, the court shall
have power to fix the time within which, and the terms upon which, the
natural or artificial persons in possession of the property the object
of the proceeding shall surrender material possession to the expro-
priating party. The court shall have power to make such orders in
respect to encumbrances, rentals, taxes, insurance and other charges,
if any, burdening the property, as shall be just and equitable. No appeal in any such cause, nor any bond or undertaking given therein,
shall operate to prevent or delay the acquisition by, or the vesting of
the title to such property in, the Administration or the Commonwealth
of Puerto Rico, as the case may be, and its material delivery thereto.

(e) In any case in which the Administration shall have acquired title in fee simple to and the possession of any land and the structures located thereon, during the course of a condemnation proceeding, before final judgment is rendered, and in which the Administration is obliged to pay the amount finally awarded as compensation, the Administration shall have power to destroy such structures erected on said land.

(f) In case of condemnation of property for the purposes of this chapter, the just compensation shall be based on the value in the market of such property, without taking into consideration any increase in such value due to the condemnation project having been announced and publicized.

The valuation to be made shall not include any increase due to well-founded and reasonable expectation that the property to be acquired by the Administration or by the Commonwealth, or other property similar thereto, or situated within the locality where the former is situated may now or later by required for public use or social benefit, or be necessary for some use to which it can be applied only by the Administration or the Commonwealth or any agency or instrumentality thereof with power for the condemnation of private property.

In case of condemnation, the just compensation shall likewise not include any new increase by reason of the public improvement or expenditures made in the locality by the Administration or the Commonwealth or any agency thereof, nor shall it include any increase by reason of any other work done by or at the initiative thereof, to effectuate the purposes of this chapter, when the increase be the result of plans or resolutions, officially adopted, for the acquisition of land for public works or for the purposes of this chapter.

(g) The provisions of sections 6-14 of Title 28 shall not apply in respect to the properties acquired by the Administration. In case of of sale of real property acquired by condemnation and no longer useful for the purpose of this chapter or for the public purposes of the Commonwealth or any of its agencies, preference shall be given to the former owners of the condemned property, or in default thereof, to their forced heirs, subject to the conditions which the Administration may establish for the sale of said property. In no case, however, shall the Administration be obliged to sell to the former owner or to his heirs at a price lower than the market value of the property in question at the time it is sold by the Administration.

When the Administration shall determine that the acquired property or any part thereof is no longer useful for the purposes of this chapter or for the public purposes of the Commonwealth or its agencies, it shall notify the person or persons from whom said property was expropriated, or the forced heirs thereof, of their preferent right to reacquire such property. The notification, showing the price and conditions of the sale offer, shall be sent by registered mail, if the addresses of the interested parties are known; if unknown, the notification shall be by edicts, published in a newspaper of general circulation once a week for two consecutive weeks. If the edict is published, it shall be presumed, subject to evidence to the contrary, that the address was unknown.

Upon expiration of the term of thirty (30) days from the notification by mail, or of forty (40) days from the publication of the last edict, which terms shall be unextendable, the Administration shall be at liberty to dispose of the property as best befits the public interest.

When the person or persons entitled to such preference accept, within the term prescribed by this action, the price and conditions of the sale, said person or persons shall be obliged to send to the Administration the amount of the value of the property, by certified check or in legal tender. If the aforesaid requisites are not complied with, acceptance of the preference shall have no validity whatsoever, and the Administration shall be entitled to dispose of the property as expressed in the preceding paragraph.

§ 311n.  Exemption from fees, taxes, registration

The properties belonging to the Administration, and any interest in any property held by it, shall be exempt from the payment of all kinds of fees, taxes (except property taxes), commonwealth or municipal tariff fees or imposts, heretofore or hereafter required by law. This exemption covers the execution of all kinds of instruments, the prosecution of proceedings of any nature, or the issuance of certifications, and recordings in the registries of property.

§ 311o.  Bonds

(a) By authority of the Government of Puerto Rico, hereby granted, the Administration may issue and sell its own bonds from time to time, and have them outstanding;

(b) The Administration, through resolution or resolutions to that effect, shall determine everything related with the date; time of maturity; rate or rates of interest; denomination or denominations; series; form; registration or conversion privileges; medium of payment; place or places of payment; terms of redemption, with or without premium; date they may be declared due, even before their maturity; replacement of mutilated, destroyed, stolen or lost bonds; and all the other conditions and stipulations which it may consider convenient;

(c) The bonds may be sold at public or private sale for such price or prices not lower than ninety-five (95) percent of the par value thereof as the Board shall determine; refunding bonds may be exchanged for outstanding bonds of the Administration on such terms as the Board may deem to be in the best interest of the Administration. All bonds of the Administration shall be negotiable instruments;

(d) The bonds of the Administration bearing the signature of the officers of the Administration in office on the date of the signing thereof, shall be valid and binding obligations, notwithstanding that before the delivery thereof and payment therefor any or all of the officers of the Administration whose signatures or facsimile signatures appear thereon have ceased to be such officers of the Administration;

(e) Temporary or interim bonds, receipts or certificates may be issued in such form and with such provisions as may be provided in such resolution or resolutions;

(f) Any resolution or resolutions authorizing bonds may contain provisions which shall be part of the contract with the bondholders: (1) as to the disposition of the entire gross or net revenue and present or future income of the Administration, including the pledging of all or any part thereof to secure payment of the bonds; (2) as to the covenant of pledging all or any part of the revenues, income or property of the Administration; (3) as to the setting aside of reserves for amortization funds, and the regulation and disposition thereof; (4) as to limitations on the purposes to which may be applied the proceeds of the sale of any issue of bonds made; (5) as to limitations on the issuance of additional bonds; (6) as to the procedure by which the terms of any resolution authorizing bonds, or any other contract with the bondholders, may be amended or abrogated; (7) as to the amount of the bonds whose holders must consent thereto, and the manner in which such consent may be given; (8) as to the events, default, and terms and conditions upon which any or all of the bonds should become or may be declared due before maturity, and as to the terms and conditions upon which such declaration and its consequences may be waived; and (9) as to any other acts or conditions which may be necessary or convenient for the security of the bonds, or that may tend to make the bonds more marketable;

(g) No officer or employee of the Administration executing bonds shall be liable personally on the bonds;

(h) The Administration is authorized to purchase any outstanding bonds issued or assumed thereby, with any funds available therefor, at a price not exceeding the principal amount or the redemption price thereof plus the accrued interest;

(i) The bonds issued by the Administration shall be lawful investments and may be accepted as securities for all trust funds,

special or public, whose investment or deposit is under the authority
and jurisdiction of the Commonwealth Government or of any officer
or employee thereof;

(j)  The bonds and other obligations issued by the Administration shall not be a debt of the Commonwealth of Puerto Rico or of any
of its agencies; nor shall such bonds or other obligations be payable
out of any funds other than those of the Administration;

(k)  The bonds issued by the Administration and the income de-
riving therefrom shall be exempt from taxes and imposts from the
Commonwealth of Puerto Rico and its agencies;

(l)  The Commonwealth of Puerto Rico does hereby pledge to,
and agree with, any of its agencies, or with any agency of the Government of the United States or of any State of the Union, or with any person subscribing to or acquiring bonds or other obligations of the Administration, that it will not encumber, limit nor restrict the properties, incomes, revenues, rights or powers hereby vested in the
Administration until all such bonds or other obligations at any time
issued, together with the interest thereon, are fully met and dis-
charged; and

(m)  In addition to the rights which they may have, subject only
to the restrictions arising from the contract, the bondholders shall
be entitled to compel the Administration, its officers, agents or employees, by mandamus, action or proceeding at law or in equity, to
fulfill any and all the terms, agreements or provisions contained in
the contract of the Administration with or for the benefit of said bondholders, and to require that there be carried out or performed any of
the resolutions and covenants of the Administration or of the duties
required by this chapter. They may likewise, by action or proceeding
at law, challenge any illegal act in violation of their rights on the part
of the Administration.

NORTH CAROLINA'S PREFERENTIAL ASSESSMENT STATUTE

§ 105-277.2. <u>Agricultural, horticultural and forest land—definitions.</u>

For the purposes of G.S. 105-277.3 through 105-277.7 the following definitions shall apply:
 (1) "Agricultural land" means land, including woodland and
     wasteland which form a contiguous part thereof, constituting
     a farm unit actively engaged in the commercial production
     of growing of crops, plants, or animals under a sound man-
     agement program.
 (2) "Forest land" means land constituting a forest unit actively
     engaged in the commercial growing of trees under a sound
     management program.
 (3) "Horticultural land" means land constituting a horticultural
     unit actively engaged in the commercial production or grow-
     ing of fruits, vegetables, nursery or floral products under a
     sound management program.
 (4) "Individually owned land (agricultural, horticultural or for-
     est)" means land, exclusive of buildings thereon, owned by
     a natural person or persons and not a corporation.
 (5) "Land" includes land and land improvements but not build-
     ings or other improvements.
 (6) "Present use value" means the price estimated in terms
     of money at which the property would change hands between
     a willing and financially able buyer and a willing seller,
     neither being under any compulsion to buy or to sell, as-
     suming that both of them have reasonable knowledge of the
     capability of the property to produce income in its present
     use and that the present use of the property is its highest
     and best use.
 (7) "Sound management program" means a program of produc-
     tion designed to obtain the greatest net return from the
     land consistent with its conservation and long-term im-
     provement. (1973, c.709, s.1.)

§ 105.277.3. <u>Agricultural, horticultural and forest land—classifica-
             tions.</u>

(a) The following classes of property are hereby designated
special classes of property under authority of Article V, Sec. 2(2)

of the North Carolina Constitution and shall be appraised, assessed and taxed as hereinafter provided:

   (1) Individually owned agricultural land, consisting of 10 acres or more and having gross income from the sale of agricultural products produced thereon (together with any payments received under a governmental soil conservation or land retirement program) averaging one thousand dollars ($1,000) per year for each of the three years immediately preceding January 1 of the year for which the benefit of this section is claimed.

   (2) Individually owned horticultural land, consisting of 10 acres or more and having gross income from the sale of horticultural products produced thereon (together with any payments received under a governmental soil conservation or land retirement program) averaging one thousand dollars ($1,000) per year for each of the three years immediately preceding January 1 of the year for which the benefit of this section is claimed.

   (3) Individually owned forest land, consisting of 20 acres or more unless the property is included in a farm unit qualifying under G.S. 105-277.3 (a)(1).

  (b) In order to come within a classification described in subdivision (a) (1), (2) or (3) above, the property must also be:

   (1) The owner's place of residence; or

   (2) Owned by the present owner, by his siblings, or by one or both of his parents for the seven years immediately preceding January 1 of the year for which the benefit of this section is claimed.

§ 105-277.4.  Agricultural, horticultural and forest land—application for taxation at present-use value.

   (a) Property coming within one of the classes defined in G.S. 105-277.3 but having a greater value for other uses shall be eligible for taxation on the basis of the value of the property in its present use if a timely and proper application is filed with the tax supervisor of the county in which the property is located. The application shall clearly show that the property comes within one of the classes and shall also contain any other relevant information required by the tax supervisor in properly appraising the property at its present-use value. The application shall be filed annually during the regular listing period. If, in the opinion of the tax supervisor, the property does not meet the requirements of this section, he shall deny the application. Decisions of the tax supervisor may be appealed to the county board of equalization and review or, if that board is not in session, to the board of county commissioners. Decisions of the county board may be appealed to the Property Tax Commission as provided in G.S. 105-324.

(b) Upon receipt of a properly executed application, the tax supervisor shall appraise the property at its present-use value as of January 1 of the year for which the application is filed. The property owner may appeal the present-use appraisal to the board of equalization and review or, if that board is not in session, to the board of county commissioners and from the county board to the Property Tax Commission. Except for valuation changes made necessary by changes in the number of acres qualified for classification or by changes in the nature of the operations of a qualifying owner, the present-use appraisal established in the year of the initial application shall continue in effect until a revaluation of all property in the county is conducted under the provisions of G.S. 105-286. If all or any part of a qualifying tract of land is located within the limits of an incorporated city or town, the tax supervisor shall furnish a copy of the property record showing both the present-use appraisal and the valuation upon which the property would have been taxed in the absence of this classification to the tax collector of the city or town. He shall also notify the tax collector of any changes in the appraisals or in the eligibility of the property for the benefit of this classification.

(c) PROPERTY MEETING THE CONDITIONS HEREIN SET FORTH SHALL BE TAXED ON THE BASIS OF THE VALUE OF THE PROPERTY FOR ITS PRESENT USE. THE DIFFERENCE BETWEEN THE TAXES DUE ON THE PRESENT-USE BASIS AND THE TAXES WHICH WOULD HAVE BEEN PAYABLE IN THE ABSENCE OF THIS CLASSIFICATION SHALL BE A LIEN ON ALL THE REAL PROPERTY OF THE TAXPAYER AS PROVIDED IN G.S. 105-355(a), SHALL BE CARRIED FORWARD IN THE RECORDS OF THE TAXING UNIT OR UNITS AS DEFERRED TAXES, BUT SHALL NOT BE PAYABLE, UNLESS AND UNTIL THE OWNER DISPOSES OF THE PROPERTY OR THE PROPERTY LOSES ITS ELIGIBILITY FOR THE BENEFIT OF THIS CLASSIFICATION FOR SOME OTHER REASON.* The tax for the fiscal year that opens in the calendar year in which a disqualification occurs shall be computed as if the property had not been classified for that year, and taxes for the preceding five fiscal years which have been deferred as provided herein, shall immediately be payable, together with interest thereon as provided in G.S. 105-360 for unpaid taxes which shall accrue on the deferred taxes due herein as if they had been payable on the dates on which they originally became due. If only a part of a qualifying tract of land loses its eligibility, a determination shall be made of the amount of deferred taxes

applicable to that part and that amount shall become payable with interest as provided above. (1973, c.709, s.1.) [*Emphasis added]

§ 105-277.5.  Agricultural, horticultural and forest land—notice of
              change in use.

Not later than the close of the listing period following a change
in use of disposal of property receiving the benefit of this classification, the property owner shall furnish the tax supervisor with complete
information regarding such change or disposal. Any property owner
who fails to notify the tax supervisor of a change in use of disposal of
a tract of land receiving the benefit of this classification shall be subject to a penalty of ten percent (10%) of the total amount of the deferred taxes and interest thereon for each listing period for which the
failure to report continues. (1973, c.709, s.1.)

§ 105-277.6.  Agricultural, horticultural and forest land—appraisal;
              computation of deferred tax.

(a) In determining the amount of the deferred taxes herein
provided, the tax supervisor shall use the appraised valuation established in the county's last general revaluation except for any changes
made under the provisions of G.S. 105-287. Such appraised valuations
shall be adjusted, however, to eliminate any economic obsolescence
allowed in the appraisal of improvements on the property on account
of the use to which the property was put at the time it was last appraised.
(b) In revaluation years, as provided in G.S. 105-286, all property entitled to classification under G.S. 105-277.3 shall be reap-
praised at its true value in money and at its present use value as of
the effective date of the revaluation. The two valuations shall continue
in effect and shall provide the basis for deferred taxes until a change
in one or both of the appraisals is required by law.
(c) To insure uniform appraisal of the classes of property
herein defined in each county, the tax supervisor shall prepare a
schedule of land values, standards and rules which, when properly
applied, will result in the appraisal of the property at its present use
value. The schedule of values, standards and rules shall be subject
to all of the conditions set forth in G.S. 105-317 (c), (c)(1) and (c)(2)
relating to the adoption of schedules, standards and rules in revaluation years. (1973, c.709, s.1.)

## DEVELOPMENT TIMING SURVEY

1. From your agency's point of view, how important are development timing problems in your agency's jurisdiction?

| 1960s | Present | 1980s | |
|-------|---------|-------|--|
| ( ) | ( ) | ( ) | our most critical problem |
| ( ) | ( ) | ( ) | a very important problem |
| ( ) | ( ) | ( ) | important, but not critical |
| ( ) | ( ) | ( ) | relatively unimportant |

2. Which of the following tools and techniques are being, or have been used in your jurisdiction in an effort to time development? Of those in use, please evaluate their effectiveness.

| | used | formerly used | intend to use | not used | | very effective | moderately effect. | slightly effect. | not effective |
|---|---|---|---|---|---|---|---|---|---|
| Large lot zoning (2+ acres) | | | | | | | | | |
| Impact zoning | | | | | | | | | |
| Agricultural zoning | | | | | | | | | |
| Down zoning | | | | | | | | | |
| Subdivision regulations | | | | | | | | | |
| Performance standards | | | | | | | | | |
| Timed development ordinances | | | | | | | | | |
| Building permit moratoria | | | | | | | | | |
| Water/Sewer extension moratoria | | | | | | | | | |
| Water/Sewer hookup moratoria | | | | | | | | | |
| Subdivision moratoria | | | | | | | | | |
| Zoning change moratoria | | | | | | | | | |

(continued)

| | used | formerly used | intend to use | not used | | very effective | moderately effect. | slightly effect. | not effective |
|---|---|---|---|---|---|---|---|---|---|
| a. Legislative – i.e., Amendments | | | | | | | | | |
| b. Administrative – i.e., Variances | | | | | | | | | |
| Development districts | | | | | | | | | |
| Urban service areas | | | | | | | | | |
| Public investment policies | | | | | | | | | |
| Preferential tax policies | | | | | | | | | |
| Public land management | | | | | | | | | |
| Transfer of development rights | | | | | | | | | |
| Land banking | | | | | | | | | |
| Other acquisition policies (specify) | | | | | | | | | |
| | | | | | | | | | |
| Others (please specify) | | | | | | | | | |
| | | | | | | | | | |

3.  There are a wide variety of objectives for which development tim-
    ing strategies are being adopted in the U.S. If your jurisdiction is
    attempting to time or phase development, please indicate those
    problems to which your strategy is directed.

    ____ Limitation of population growth
    ____ Control of rate of population growth
    ____ Provision of adequate urban services
    ____ Reduction of urban sprawl
    ____ Reduction of traffic congestion
    ____ Prevent overcrowding of schools
    ____ Control housing costs
    ____ Environmental protection
    ____ Environmental enhancement
    ____ Preservation of open space
    ____ Preserve local amenities
    ____ Preserve character of community
    ____ Reduce speculation in private land market
    ____ Protect property values
    ____ Improve governmental financial stability
    ____ Lower tax rates
    ____ Others (specify)

    ____

4.  For those tools or techniques which you have rated as being rela-
    tively ineffective, please briefly explain why you think this is so.


5.  What changes to do you see as necessary for more effective tim-
    ing of development in your jurisdiction?


6.  Has there been any strong political reaction resulting from your
    agency's attempts to time development? If so, please give details.


7.  Has there been any litigation resulting from your agency's at-
    tempts to time development? If so, please give details.


8.  To what extent are your development timing efforts directly co-
    ordinated with state and/or regional plans or standards? Please
    give details.

DAVID J. BROWER is the Director of Urban Services in the Center for Urban and Regional Studies and the Coordinator of the Combined Degree Program in Law and Planning at the University of North Carolina at Chapel Hill. A lawyer and a planner, he is a graduate of the University of Michigan and the University of Michigan Law School. He has been admitted to practice law in Illinois, Indiana, Michigan and before the Supreme Court of the United States; he is a member of the American Institute of Planners. He is a coeditor (with Randall Scott and Dallas Miner) of Management and Control of Growth, published by the Urban Land Institute, Washington, D.C.

DAVID W. OWENS is an attorney on the land policy staff of the Wisconsin State Planning Office. Mr. Owens received his M.R.P. and J.D. degrees from the University of North Carolina, where he was a student in the Combined Degree Program in Law and Planning. He has also studied English Planning Law at Oxford University. Mr. Owens' other publications include books and articles on the legal aspects of public access to recreational beaches and public participation in land use planning and decision making.

RONALD H. ROSENBERG is an Attorney-Advisor for the Office of Legislation, Environmental Protection Agency in Washington, D.C. He is a graduate of the Combined Degree Program in Law and Planning at the University of North Carolina at Chapel Hill. Mr. Rosenberg has published law review articles in the areas of coastal zone management, the Federal-Aid Highway Program, and prison reform.

IRA J. BOTVINICK is a student at the University of North Carolina in the Combined Degree Program in Law and Planning, working towards the M.R.P. and J.D. degrees. Mr. Botvinick has been elected to the University of North Carolina Law Review and is a member of the Moot Court Bench. He has worked for the Advisory Commission on Housing and Urban Growth of the American Bar Association and the North Carolina Office of State Planning.

MICHAEL S. MANDEL is currently Director and Counsel, Urban Governmental Affairs, for the National Association of Home Builders.
Before joining NAHB, Mr. Mandel was a Research Associate with the Land Use Center of the Urban Institute in Washington, D.C.

He received J.D. and M.R.P. degrees from the University of North Carolina at Chapel Hill under the Combined Degree Program in Law and Planning.

Mr. Mandel is the editor of Local Government Affairs and co-editor of State and Urban Reporter, both NAHB publications. He is also a contributing editor to NAHB's Journal-Scope. His most recent article is "Mistaking the Taking Issue," published in ASPO's Land Use Law and Zoning Digest.

LAND BANKING IN THE CONTROL OF URBAN
DEVELOPMENT
>
Harvey L. Flechner

SYSTEMATIC URBAN PLANNING
>
Darwin G. Stuart

URBAN NONGROWTH: Planning for People
>
Earl Finkler, William J. Toner,
and Frank J. Popper

URBAN PROBLEMS AND PUBLIC POLICY
CHOICES
>
edited by Joel Bergsman
and Howard L. Wiener

THE EFFECTS OF URBAN GROWTH: A Popu-
lation Impact Analysis
>
Richard P. Appelbaum, Jennifer A.
Bigelow, Henry P. Kramer, Harvey L.
Molotch, and Paul Relis

EXCLUSIONARY ZONING: Land Use Regulation
and Housing in the 1970s
>
Richard F. Babcock
and Fred P. Bosselman

LAND USE, OPEN SPACE, AND THE GOVERN-
MENT PROCESS: The San Francisco Bay Area
Experience
>
edited by Edward Ellis Smith
and Durward S. Riggs